Aug 8/80

Dear Paul

In Solidarity

Sr. Mary Jackson

CREDITS

"Towards Total Liberation," "Who is Mary?" and "Go Tell Everyone" come from the *Proceedings of the Asian Women's Consultation*. 1987.
"A Ritual of Completion and Separation" is adapted from the ritual of Florence Perella Hayes.
"Remembering and Bequest" and "A Ritual of Completion and Separation" are adapted from *Women Church: Theology and Practice of Feminist Liturgical Communities* by Rosemary Radford Reuther.
"Covenant Celebration for WICCA" is adapted from *Rite of Naming* by Kate Pravera.
"Celebrating a Women's Book" is taken from rituals by Rachel C. Wahlberg and Ann M. Heidkamp in *Ecumenical Decade 1988-98 Churches in Solidarity with Women*, a publication of the World Council of Churches.

Cover photo of "Women Going to Church," painted by Damian Domingo. courtesy of Ayala Museum
Design Consultation by **R. PETER L. CUASAY**

Grateful appreciation is extended to **LINA SAGARAL REYES, FE MANGAHAS, OPHELIA S. REYES, ANGELITO PINEDA, LILIA PINEDA, RIQUI NUNEZ,** De La Salle University Press and Pima Printing Press.

Special thanks to **ELMER MENDOZA, LHAI & PHINES MANALILI, ROLAND DE GUZMAN, JUN REYES, VAL MAÑALÀC, DAVE ROTONI, RIC PINEDA, LHEN MAGAT, OFEL SANGIL, OGIE NUCUM, ARVIN PINEDA, BERNIE FLORES** and **FRANCIS BALTAZAR.**

PRODUCTION EDITOR: **PIA CRISOSTOMO ARBOLEDA**

WOMAN
AND RELIGION

A Collection of
Essays, Personal Histories, and
Contextualized Liturgies

SR. MARY JOHN MANANZAN, OSB, Editor

The Institute of Women's Studies
St. Scholastica's College
Manila
1988

TABLE OF CONTENTS

Chapter 1   **OLD TEXTS, NEW IMAGES**

WOMAN AND RELIGION

FOREWORD

In constructing a building, laying down the second stone is almost as important as laying down the cornerstone. Similarly, producing the second volume of a series is almost as important as publishing the first because it seems to guarantee the continuation of the series. Thus, it is with great joy that we present the second book in our Women's Studies Series.

Yet *Woman and Religion* is no mere sequel; it is, like its predecessor, another major contribution to local materials for women. It delves into women's perspectives of religion, for religion plays an integral role in women's lives. Religion is taken as a system of thought, a cultural institution, and a ritual structure. Thus the book has three parts. The first section provides a theoretical framework; the second part gathers testimony on the negative and positive influences of religion on lives of women from different backgrounds; the third portion documents liturgical services that consciously take a women's perspective.

The first article, entitled "Woman and Religion," introduces the different aspects of the theme. Like an overture, it provides an overview and a common thread running through what might otherwise seem to be a diversity of topics.

Having gotten a glimpse of the terrain in the first article, the second piece by Grace Tirona makes a critical delineation of the image of women in Hinduism, Buddhism, and Mohammedanism. Susan Evangelista goes into greater detail by discussing the image of women in Hindu literature.

The theme continues in a specifically Christian key. Arche Ligo presents a general discussion on the images and roles of women in the Bible, both Old and New Testaments. Still from a Biblical context, Sr. Helen Graham shows how actual Biblical exegesis could be done from a women's perspective and how such an interpretation can empower contemporary women towards the pursuit of peace in our day. Sr. Hilda Buhay's article explores the positive and negative aspects of the influence and importance of Mary in the spirituality of Filipino women.

In the last four articles of chapter one, there is an evident effort not only to discern in religion the oppressive factors weighing on people in general, and women in particular, but to further discover the liberating forces that could inspire dedicated lives. The reformulation of salvation is seen as an integral process of liberation from concrete evils and a working out of concrete blessings. This vision has been shown to motivate people in the struggle to make this society more humane and to eradicate oppression or exploitation due to class, race, or sex. It has actually enabled Church women to bring about a new ecumenism that does not "come from above" in doctrinal definitions or liturgical principles, but from the depth of basic experiences and the common struggle against oppression. And as people go through the crucible of suffering to reorient their faith, the change begins to be reflected in the efforts of women to systematize their theological insights and contribute to Third World theologizing by adding their own Asian Women's perspective.

The second chapter expands the personal basis of the new ecumenism by gathering several experiential accounts of the common struggle. The attempt to document the experiences of women as they go through life in search of meaning was inspired by the contributions of our students in our course "Woman and Religion." Since some aspects of the personal histories may affect people who are still very much alive, most of the authors have opted to use pen names.

The final section of the book is a collection of prayers and liturgical services which we have actually used in the celebration of important moments of our lives, personal and social. They are significant entries, not so much because they highlight these moments, but because they consciously attempt to use inclusive language, a concrete step towards systematizing and internalizing theological insights born of experiences and struggle.

No single book can cover all the aspects of the question of woman and religion. But if, as a second volume in a broad series, one book can stimulate discussion on this very important aspect in the women's struggle, our aim will have been realized. May this beginning also inspire us to already affect some changes suggested by the agenda of Church renewal mentioned in one of the articles. In spite of the tremendous obstacles, we live in hope, emboldened by the aphorism: "Trust in God. SHE will provide."

Sr. Mary John Mananzan, OSB, ed.
Malate, April 1988

old texts,
new images

WOMAN AND RELIGION

Sr. Mary John Mananzan, OSB

Introduction

The root of women's oppression in religions was recognized in an ecumenical consultation of Church women held in Manila in November 1985 and attended by participants from seven Asian countries. They wrote in their composite statement:

> As Church people, we have come to realize that the highly patriarchal churches have definitely contributed to the subjugation and marginalization of women. Thus we see an urgent need to re-examine our Church structures, traditions, and practices in order to remedy injustice and to correct misinterpretations and interpretations and distortions that have crippled us.
>
> We saw how Theology itself has added to these distortions. We unearthed theological premises, traditions, and beliefs that have prevented us from becoming fully human and have blurred the image of God that we are. [1]

This is corroborated by Denise Lardner Carmody who writes:

> Beyond doubt, major religions of the world have a dubious record with regard to women... For example, Buddhist women could not head the religious community. Hinduism usually held women ineligible for salvation. Islam made a woman's witness only half that of a man. Christianity called a woman the weaker vessel, the more blurred image of the Image. Jewish men blessed God for not having made them women. [2]

There was, however, an equal conviction that there are liberating forces in religion. Whether oppression or liberation, there is no doubt about the tremendous effect of religion on women. Much of women's self and social image is derived from religious values. Thus a study of religions is of the utmost importance for women's self-understanding of their situation. There is a need "to winnow the wheat of authentic religion... from the religious sexist chaff."[3] This paper will confine itself to the reflection on women and the Christian religion.

The Goddess Cult

One of the problematic issues in religion that affects women is the prevailing male notion of God. It is interesting to go into the roots of the formation of this male God's image because before patriarchal monotheism, religions existed with a Goddess as dominant divine image or together with a male God. It must be a surprise to Christians of today to find out that the most ancient human image of God was, as archeology shows, female.

Rosemary Radford Ruether, in her book *Sexism and God Talk*, describes one of the different forms of these goddesses, the Goddess of fertility:

> *Their figures typically emphasize the breasts, buttocks, and enlarged abdomen of the female; hands and legs are given little attention. This suggests that the Goddess is not a focus of personhood, but rather an impersonalized image of the mysterious power of fecundity.*[4]

There is also the Primal Matrix form, the great womb which generates all other forms of creation. In Sumer and Babylon, the Goddess is paired with male gods. A corresponding sacerdotal class of both male and female members, preside over the cultic sacrifices. But there is no complementarity involved in this pairing of male and female forms of God. Rather there was an equality.

There is also the famous Goddess Isis in Egyptian religion whose cult encompassed the ancient Mediterranean world. This Goddess incorporated in herself the characteristics of other goddesses. She could cure the sick, raise the dead; she gifted nations with language and astronomy, the art of weaving, painting, etc. She is also full of mercy and compassion and is sometimes considered the precursor of the Mary-cult of Christianity.[5]

The great oriental religions also had female forms of God. Hinduism has a tradition of the Great Goddess religion which worshipped a female divinity under many names and forms. Denise Carmody describes some of these forms:

> For instance there is Saramya, "she who runs." Saramya rushes into creation as untamed creative will. She is a model for human life, as mother of both Death and the Asvins (twin saviors born to heal humanhood's ills). Then there is Saramya who outwits the demons that stole away light and reestablishes cosmic order. Third, the Goddess appears as Sarasvati, the daughter of lightning and voice of thunder, who grants human flashes of insight... Like the river, she rushes into human consciousness, the well-spring of intuition and creativity... Further, the Vedas tell of Aditi, boundless Mother of all. As boundless she is androgyne: Mother, father and all gods, being, non-being,whatever is or will be born... As Vedism became a highly priestly religion, and assumed that inerrant ritual performances guaranteed cosmic order and forced the god's will, Aditi became very important. Somewhat related to this is Vak the goddess who controlled all speech. Vak, conceived the Creator and gave birth without male help. She was the parthogenic, womblike source of cosmic order, the Godhead and author, through revelation to seers and sages, of the Vedas–the external world.[6]

In Philippine history there are no traditions of women goddesses.However,it is significant to note that the word for God, *Bathala*, does not have a sexist connotation. In the primitive Tagalog script, the word "god" is made up of three consonants *Ba-Tha-La*. The first consonant is the first syllable of the word *babae* (woman) which symbolizes generation. The third consonant is the first syllable of *lalake* (man) which symbolizes potency. They are joined by the middle consonant, an aspirated H which means light or spirit. The word "god", therefore, means the union of man and woman in light. And when one reads the word backwards, it reads *Lahatba*, meaning total generation, total creator ("to do", "creador"). In other words, the concept of god among the ancient Tagalogs was more closely linked with woman; and, when linked with both the concepts of man and woman, there is a nuance of union and mutuality, not subordination.

There are also Filipino legends concerning *diwatas*,

such as that of Maria Makiling who was supposed to inhabit a mountain and who brought peace, calm, order and well-being in the community.

The point of this discussion is to establish the fact that the male god image, which is taken for granted in Judaeo-Christian culture evolved in a certain period of history during the establishment of patriarchal monotheism and is therefore not true of all times and of all cultures, but is actually "a sharp departure from all previous human consciousness."[7]

Women and the Christian Bible

Throughout the history of the Church until now the Bible has been used to justify the subordination and discrimination of women, and yet women, not men, are the most constant believers in the Bible or God's word.

First, it has to be noted that the Bible was written in a patriarchal society. Although its authors are unknown, the books of the Bible have been attributed to men writers, have been interpreted by men and have been taught for the last two thousand years by men.

In the monotheistic patriarchalism of the Hebrews, God was considered a patriarch. There was a pronounced male domination over woman. It had a double standard of morality favorable to men. Women were considered properties of their fathers or husbands. The women's main contribution was bearing children. That was why to be barren was a curse. Needless to say, they were excluded from cultic participation except as spectators. They had to observe ritual purification for menstruation and childbirth.

However, in spite of these limitations, prominent women emerged in the Old Testament. There was Deborah, the mighty prophetess; Esther, who saved her people; Ruth, a symbol of fidelity; Judith, who was considered an honor of her people and the glory of Israel; Delilah, Thamar, etc.

The movement that Jesus of Nazareth initiated was a movement critical to the then prevailing Jewish society. Elizabeth Fiorenza writes:

> As a renewal movement the Jesus movement stands in conflict with its Jewish society and is "heretical" with respect to the Jewish religious community. The

*earliest Jesus traditions expect a reversal of all social
conditions through the eschatological intervention of
God; this is initially realized in the ministry of Jesus.
Therefore the Jesus movement can accept all those
who, according to contemporary social standards are
marginal people and who are, according to the Torah,
"unclean": the poor, the exploited, the public sinners,
the publicans, the maimed and sick, and last but not
the least, the women.*[8]

Therefore, it is not surprising that Jesus' treatment of
women went against the accustomed attitude of the Jews.
Jesus took women seriously and chose them as disciples and
primary witnesses; for example, Mary Magdalene and the
three women who witnessed the empty tomb. He not only
talked publicly with the Samaritan woman, he even engaged
her in a theological discussion and revealed his mission to
her. He was forgiving of the woman taken in adultery and put
up the Syro-Phoenician woman as a model of faith. He gave
his Mother, Mary, a significant role in his mission.

In the early Christian communities, the character of the
Jesus movement found expression in the abolition of social
distinctions of class, religion, race and gender. (Gal. 3:28)
Gentiles, slaves and women assumed leadership functions in
the missionary activities. Prisca, for example, together with
her husband Aquilles played an important role equal to St.
Paul's. So did Thecla and Lydia, and other women who
played prominent roles in the development of the early
Christian communities.

Unfortunately, the egalitarian elements in the Jesus
movement gradually got eliminated in what Elizabeth
Fiorenza calls "ecclesiastical patriarchalization". This was a
part of the "apologetic development of cultural adaptation
that was necessary because the early Christian missionary
movement, like the Jesus movement in Palestine, was a
counter-cultural conflict movement that undermined the
patriarchal structure of the Graeco-Roman politeia."[9]

This ecclesiastical patriarchalization led to the exclusion
of women from church offices; women had to conform to their
stereotyped role in patriarchal culture. It was no longer
woman's call to discipleship that wrought out her salvation
but her prescribed role as wife and mother.

Women in Church History

The ecclesiastical patriarchalization went on relentlessly throughout Church history. The Fathers of the Church reacting against Gnosticism, which allowed the female principle in its concept of the godhead, became increasingly misogynistic in their writings. Tertullian, for example, lashed out against Gnostic women as "heretical, bold and immodest because they presumed to prophesy, teach, exercise and baptize." [10] To him is attributed the harsh words addressing women:

> Women, you ought to dress yourselves in mourning and rags, representing yourself as penitents bathed in tears, redeeming thus the fault of having ruined the human race. You are the door of hell; you corrupt him whom the devil dare not approach; you finally, are the cause why Jesus Christ had to die. [11]

Origen castrated himself because he believed marital relations lessened the efficacy of prayer. St. John Chrysostom blamed woman for the sins of David and Solomon and described woman as a storehouse of spittle and phlegm. Augustine avowed: "I know nothing which brings the manly mind down from the height more than a woman's caresses and that joining of bodies without which one cannot have a wife." [12]

The doctors of the Church were no better. Thomas Aquinas considered women as "misbegotten males" Gracian propounded:

> Different kinds of temptations make war on man in his various ages, some when he is young and others when he is old; but woman threatens him perpetually. Neither the youth, nor the adult, nor the old man, nor the wise, nor the brave, nor even the saint is ever safe from woman. [13]

Because of this there was a significant stress on vowed celibacy both for men and women. With the establishment of monasteries, a communal life of celibates with the vows of poverty, chastity and obedience took form. With time, convent life became circumscribed by the rules imposed by clerical authorities who are, of course, male. In the sixth century they prescribed the cloister for all nuns which was to be kept strictly.

In the Middle Ages there emerged a systematic persecution of charismatic women who were condemned as witches. In 1484 a tract was published entitled Malleus Maleficarum (The Hammer Against Witches) which was an anthology of the product of fevered imaginations regarding the alleged habits, characteristics, and evil techniques of females given over to Satan. Between the 13th-18th centuries, about a million women including Joan of Arc were burned to death as witches.

In spite of this, some women of the Middle Ages broke through the repressive situation into the limelight like Juliana of Norwich, a famous mystic; St. Gertrude, St. Mechtilde and St. Therese of Avila who were famous for their scholarship; and St. Catherine of Siena who had tremendous influence on popes and bishops in important ecclesiastical matters.

The Protestant Revolution that did a lot to promote the role of the laity failed to do the same for women. In fact by restraining devotion to Mary and by suppressing the convents, the Reformation removed several of women's safety valves. Even Martin Luther was ambivalent about women. He failed to see the sexism in biblical patriarchalism. He still preached that the role of women was procreation and nurturing. However, the emerging Lutheran and Calvinist Churches did recognize the social and theological role of women. They accepted women preachers in the 17th century. The Quakers recognized sexual equality and produced great women preachers like Elizabeth Houton, Mary Dyer and Elizabeth Fry.

In the 19th century Mary Baker Eddy founded Christian Science and renewed the Father-Mother image of God. Likewise, Catholic women of the counter-reformation such as Angela Merici, Louise de Marillac, etc. broke through the restrictions to engage in social services.

In the 20th century, with the advent of the feminist movement, the emancipation of women in the Church sees its first real glimmer of hope.

Women in Philippine Church History

The Pre-Spanish Filipino Society cannot be called matriarchal but the Filipino women did enjoy equal status with the male. Equal value was given to male or female off-spring. The *mujer indigena* received equal inheritance; her training was the same as her male counterpart. The wife enjoyed the same right as the husband in marriage including the right to divorce. She participated in managing the domestic economy as well as in agricultural production. She could be a "pact holder" which shows equality in political leadership opportunities. She had a pre-eminent role in religious cult being the priestess, *babaylan*, who offered sacrifices in all the important events celebrated by the community.

In the 16th century, Spain brought Christianity and Western Civilization with its patriarchal society to the Philippines. The same misogynistic trend that was present in the Western Church was, of course, brought to the island as is shown in the following instruction to parish priests in the colony:

> *Woman is the most monstrous animal in the whole of nature, bad tempered and worse spoken. To have this animal in the house is asking for trouble in the way of tattling, talebearing, malicious gossip and controversies, for wherever a man is, it would seem to be impossible to have peace and quiet. However, even this might be tolerated if it were not for the danger of unchastity. Not only should the parish priest of Indians abstain from employing any woman in his house, but he should not allow them to enter it, even if they are only paying a call.*[14]

The friars spared no effort to mold the Filipino women to the image and likeness of the Spanish women of the Iberian society of their time where their lifestyle did not differ much from that of a contemplative nun of today. Schools for girls were established, and manuals for young girls were translated to engrain in young girls the values, concepts and prescriptions of the friars. The cult of the Blessed Virgin Mary was introduced to complete their domestication. (There is of course a liberating way of honoring Mary.)

The product of this friar education was later personified in the sweet, shy, docile, and pious Maria Clara, the heroine of Jose Rizal's novel, *Noli Me Tangere*.

Later on, during the Propaganda movement, the ilustrados who were trying to awaken the national consciousness of the people denounced the friars' sexual exploitation of Filipino women and their domestication that Spanish religious education had effected. In spite of these massive efforts to subdue the Filipino women, individuals broke through the mold in different epochs of history like Gabriela Silang, Tandang Sora, Gregoria de Jesus, etc. An interesting example is that of an unnamed woman during the Ilocos Revolt who dared to preach against the Parish Priest who made the indignant denunciation:

> Last Sunday, I preached again to the people exhorting them to their obligation and vassalage to the sovereign so that those who have remained faithful until then would maintain their sentiment without prevarication. While I was preaching, a woman had the nerve to also preach saying that they should not believe me, that everything I said were lies and that in the name of God and the Gospel, we do nothing but deceive them so that we Spaniards could fleece them, well we (the friars) are also Spaniards like all the others.[15]

But apart from the individual women who have defied their domestication and in spite of the growth of the women's movement even among church women, the great majority have internalized the stereotyped roles Church and society have assigned to them.

Women in the Church Today

This section will have to treat separately the Protestant and the Catholic Churches. It will also discuss the matter taking into consideration the teachings, the practices, the structure and the ritual of the Churches.

The Catholic Church still holds a rather conservative view of women. Church teachings on family life still emphasize the "obey your husband" dictum. It allows only the natural methods of family planning and has not lifted its ban on divorce.

Its moral theology still focuses on the "sins of the flesh" with a certain bias against women as "Eve, the tempress". It offers the model of Mary as Virgin-Mother which is rather difficult for Catholic women to emulate.

The heirarchy refuses to take the ordination of women seriously even if progressive theologians find no fundamental reasons for the discrimination. In spite of the fact that women are the most active in Church service functions and activities, they are deprived of participation in the major decision-making processess. Celibate priests continue, in fact, to make the rules and prescriptions governing marriage and family life. The structure is hierarchical and clerical, and women have no part in both.

In the Liturgy, there is still a sexist tone addressing the assembly as "brethren" praying for the salvation of "mankind" and exhorting to love one's "fellowmen." The women are given minor roles in the liturgy but they shoulder the more burdensome preparations behind the scenes and the "making order" after each celebration.

In spite of the lack of legal authority, however, religious women have a vital role in the Church. In the Philippines they enjoy a credibility among the faithful which surpasses that of the priests. They are also among the most conscientized and are active in groups and peoples' organizations that are in solidarity with the struggle of the poor and the oppressed. Lately they have become aware of themselves as women concerned with the "woman question" and are contributing to the emancipation of their sisters towards a full development of their personhood.

The structure of Protestant Churches is less hierarchical than that of the Roman Catholic Church. Bishops are elected and pastors are petitioned by the parishioners. There is normally a National Conference where the laity is represented in the decision-making. In some protestant denominations there is already ordination of women pastors. However in actual church practice there are still many things left to be desired. I will let Protestant women speak for themselves. Ruth Kao writes:

> *"There is a Women's Department Secretary in the working of the main assembly of the Church... In the local Church we have women deaconesses and for about fifty years we have had women ministers. But there are very few women in the decision-making bodies of the Presbytary or the Assembly. But we are now educating ourselves to be more self-reliant and to encourage our women to take part in these activities."*16

Audrey Rebera, Associate General Secretary of the Student Christian Movement in Sri Lanka shares her views:

About two years ago, the Methodist Church accepted the ordination of women and right now at the Lanks Theological College they have about four or five women candidates for the ministry. They have already ordained two deaconesses into the full ministry of the Church. These two women perform as full time pastors of their Churches. Since their involvement with the Church has been a long standing one, their acceptance in the role of pastor was an easy transition. However a great deal of new ground will have to be broken by the new candidates when they go into the pastoral role. This is in some ways an unequal expectation because there are higher expectations from the women than people have of the male candidates.[17]

Saramma Jacob of the Syrian Orthodox Church of India pinpoints the problems of women in her Church:

"Women in our Church have two urgent problems. They are 1) to have voting right in the Church, 2) to be admitted to theological seminaries. Though women are faithful in worship they do not have equal rights with men in the Church. Men believe that they represent women as well. Regarding entering seminaries, there is a belief that women do not need theology."[18]

Cynthia Lam, Women's Secretary of the Hongkong Christian Council laments:

"In the Church,women play a traditional role, preparing Holy Communion. Women's opinions are not respected. They are not taken into consideration. Women are expected to be obedient to the leaders and not to speak up. But it is the women who teach Sunday school, prepare the worship and do home visitations. Although there are more women than men in most congregations, there are more men than women in decision-making bodies. So in practice the minority lead the majority."[19]

Efforts at Renewal: The Feminist Theology of Liberation

It is not enough to analyze the situation of women in the churches or to pinpoint the roots of women's oppression in religion. It is imperative that out of this analysis, efforts must be exerted to remedy the situation through participation in women's movements. Women trained in theology must also re-think the discipline itself and bring about a transformation within the churches. Hence, the feminist theology of liberation. Rosemary Ruether delineates the critical principles of such a theology:

> The critical principle of feminist theology is the promotion of the full humanity of women; whatever denies, diminishes, distorts the full humanity of women is, therefore, appraised as not redemptive. Theologically speaking, whatever diminishes or denies the full humanity of woman must be presumed not to reflect the divine or an authentic relation to the divine nor to reflect the authentic nature of things, nor to be the message or work of an authentic redeemer or the community of redemption. This negative principle also implies the positive principle: What does promote the full humanity of women is of the Holy, it does reflect true relation to the divine, it is the true nature of the thing, the authentic message of redemption and the mission of redemptive community. [20]

The agenda of renewal must include all aspects of theology: from the re-interpretation of scriptures, to the historical-critical reflection of Church doctrine from the women's point of view, to the re-discovery of the great women of Church history, to the fundamental questioning of the Church's hierarchical structure, its constricting prescriptions, its discriminatory practices and the sexist language of its liturgy.

These will lead to the stripping away of women's false consciousness, freeing them to discover themselves and their potentials and to come to their full blossoming. In the running over of this bliss, they, together with all peoples of God, will use their energy towards the transformation of society into a "new heaven and a new earth."

ENDNOTES

[1]From the Proceedings of the Asian Women Consultation (Manila 1985) p. 221.

[2]Denise Lardner Carmody, *Women and World Religious.* (Nashville: The Pantheon Press, 1979), p. 14.

[3]Ibid.

[4]Rosemary R. Reuther, *Sexism and God Talk -- Towards a Feminist Theology.* (Boston: Beacon Press, 1983), p. 48

[5]Christa Mulah, *Maria.--die Geheime Gottin in Christent.*

[6]Carmody, p. 41.

[7]Reuther, p. 53.

[8]Elizabeth Fiorenza "You are not to be called Father: Early History in a Feminist Perspective." *Cross Currents* 29/3 (1979), p. 315.

[9]Ibid., p. 316.

[10]Carmody, p. 120.

[11]Quoted in M.J. Mananzan, "The Filipino Woman" in *Essays on Women,* (Manila: St. Scholastica's College Institute of Women's Studies, 1987), p. 22.

[12]Quoted in Carmody, p. 122.

[13]Quoted in C.R. Boxer. *Mary Misogymy* (London, Duchworth 1975), p. 100.

[14]Casimiro Diaz, quoted in Sr. Mary John Mananzan, *Essays On Women.* P. 27.

[15]Apuntes Interesantes sobre las Islas Filipinas por un Español de larga experiencia en el pais y amante del progreso. (Madrid, 1870), p. 59.

[16]Ruth Kao, Quoted in "Emerging Patterns in the Women's Movement in Asia", *God's Images.* Dec. 85/Feb. 86, p. 15-16.

[17]Ibid, p. 17-18.

[18]Ibid, p. 22.

[19]Ibid, p. 24.

[20]Reuther, pp. 18-19.

IMAGES OF WOMAN IN ASIAN RELIGIONS

Mary Grace Ampil-Tirona

The story of the origin and spread within Asian territories of Hinduism, Buddhism and Islam reveals the extent to
which religious forces are intertwined with the region's political and socio-economic realities. In turn, these factors have
converged to buttress a most potent psychological rationale
that has determined woman's status in Asian society -- the
defense of the male ego.

Historical Considerations

Hinduism is indigenous to India. It has had no appeal
elsewhere since the religion sprang from peculiar social
needs. Through an elaborate belief system, Hinduism was
used to entrench upper caste, specifically Brahmanic and
male, superiority over the rest of the social and sexual strata.
The latter included nobles, merchants, farmers, and an
assortment of lesser occupational groupings of ill-repute such
as butchers, street sweepers, undertakers, etc.

Buddhism started as a protest school of Hinduism and
was designed to undermine Brahmanic impositions on the
conduct of daily life. With a relatively simplified belief system
that emphasized egalitarianism and salvation from desire and
worldly existence, it found a wider appeal outside the land of
its birth and moved on to East and Southeast Asia.

Islam has been perceived as a religion of conquest since
it sought to liberate through a theocratic tradition of order.
Like Buddhism, it gained a wide following in the Asian hemi-
sphere due to its emphasis on the fraternity of men, a universal ideal which was sowed through political means.

The motley of ideas, beliefs and principles that have been
popularized as Hindu, Buddhist and Islamic is the product of

the collective effort of numerous scholars, lawgivers and priests. However, it is not surprising to find their occasional ingenuous attribution to so-called religious founders or gods. In fact, Hinduism has no acknowledged founder. Buddha, while an authentic historical personality, cannot be accurately traced as the author of statements and writings as claimed in various sources. Being a mere camel driver, Mohammed has no reputable standing as a scholar although he is an acknowledged founder. Nevertheless, the claim persists that the Koran constitutes divine revelation.

What can safely be asserted then is that none of these religions' originators have claimed or have been made to claim divine descent. Human authorship notwithstanding, the emergent body of writings have become tradition and law, both prescriptive and normative in intent. Interestingly enough, a common underlying thread is their male fountainhead — a truly man-made corpus of ideals, exclusively for the protection and preservation of the well-being of their own kind.

Sociological Preconditions

Unpopular as the idea may seem, environmental determinism is a key to the understanding of woman's image and eventual treatment in Asian society. A quick scanning of the milieu where countless women continue to struggle for survival and protection, not to mention recognition as equal to man, will show a geographically and historically fragmented scenario. Strangely enough, life in such a harsh nomadic-agrarian economy, where divisive conquests have been endemic, has aggravated the lot of womankind while at the same time purportedly enhancing their role in society. This, of course, is all a matter of point of view.

The assignment of value to woman has largely been a function of genetics, economics, religion, and culture. Woman was vested with procreative or reproductive utility necessary for the pleasure and propagation of mankind. Her productive labor services on the home and farming fronts freed her menfolk for what was perceived as the more vital responsibilities of defense, conquest and communal administration. In other instances, she was a valuable commodity, an easy-to-produce "self-made" gift item that imbued the social relationships of exchanging males with the highest of personal considerations. As a hearth-bound transmitter of customs and tradition in the course of bringing up children, she helped perpetuate an untainted cultural heritage that reinforced her own servitude. And in the context of societies where sexuality has been dignified as a sacred duty of man, she was the vital instrument in the fulfillment of his religious obligation. For example, *Kama* or the pursuit of physical pleasure was a Hindu's *Dharma* or duty in tandem with *Artha* or the achievement of wealth and worldly advantage.

The fluctuation of woman's value was the inevitable consequence of an unstable and uncontrollable social order. Demographic uncertainties arose to determine her social price as the law of supply and demand would dictate. This resulted in varying degrees of control ranging from complete segregation and restriction to the extreme of sale, gift give-away or outright infanticide. Status and treatment were prescribed by diverse roles and duties assigned to daughter, wife, mother, widow; divorcee, slave, courtesan, prostitute, temptress; bodhisattva (saint), nun, scholar, philosopher, warrior, sorceress, caliph. The rationalizations or interpretations of the respective importance — more or less — as were attached to these categories of women depended on the exigencies of the times. Often enough, the major consideration was whatsoever suited the male ego best. In many instances, the promotion of family continuity and stability, or of children and women's welfare, were convincing arguments that kept woman in willing bondage. Political circumstances such as threats from invaders, marauders, kidnappers or slave traders compounded the restrictions into a somewhat positive defensive measure for the benefit of womankind.

Thus it has been suggested in various sources that in the early stages of Asian history, woman was treated liberally. She was considered educable, if not given the privilege of joining the ranks of scholars and priests. Marriage was a free choice on her part, during which she was both friend and equal partner. As wife and mother, she was highly esteemed. Monogamy was the norm, and thus marriage was indissoluble. Illegitimacy was protected, while widowhood was dignified so as to prevent remarriage. The Upanishadic literature of Hinduism lends to the truth of male-female equality by treating creation as impelled by the necessity of partnership between the sexes, i.e., One alone, the Creator was inadequate and caused a fall into two pieces — a she-god and a he-god — after which all the beings of creation were made by the assumption first of a female and then a male form.

With the growth of communities as well as the frequency and intensity of conflicts between invading hordes and settled agrarian folk, social and political life increased in complexity. From the second millenium BC onwards, the treatment of woman was confused and confounded by a welter of constricting practices. The right of choice was substituted by arranged marriages at the onset of puberty. Bride gifting at an ever lowering age revealed the pressure to ensure the bethrotal and security of one's daughter at the earliest possible time. This was resorted to either as a value protecting mechanism or as a sheer defensive reaction against marauding forces and slave traders. In time, rearing a daughter was seen not only as hazardous and disadvantageous, but also as an outflow of resources, and eventually, a burden to the point of disgrace. Increased pressure to pass on a daughter as soon and as cheaply as possible institutionalized polygamy which, under the circumstances, can be seen as a response to economic forces. Bereft of choice on her marital fate, pressured into reproductive utility, disgraced if left to fend on her own— woman was forced into accepting the practice of supercession or replacement in the event of barrenness. Eventually, this also meant that her husband was lord, master and god—to be treated loyally and respectfully regardless of his worth. Following these were other untenable but tolerated impositions such as the prescriptions on divorce, loss of equal inheritance rights, and prohibitions against voluntary giftgiving, selling or business involvement, and adultery. Perhaps, the only light at the end of the dark tunnel in which woman found herself unwillingly secluded was her protection against abandonment in the event of supercession.

Perceptions Arising from Male-Female Dynamics

Hindu writings did not fail to discern the imminent dangers of unbridled female sexuality or the particularly libidinous nature of women that could render their womenfolk unmarriageable and thus, a disgrace and an economic liability to the family. However, it is in Buddhist religious literature, authored by venerable monks, that one finds candid admissions of the weakness of man in the face of inherently sensuous woman. For unlike Hinduism with its prescriptions for a hierarchical-functional social and therefore sexual order, Buddhism claimed to uphold the egalitarian ideal in all forms and circumstances. Thus we find seemingly contradictory assertions by self-serving monks regarding male-female distinctions on the one hand, and arguments upholding the distinction-less a sexual ideal as ultimately reconciled in the Buddhahood on the other. In Buddhism, there was an apparent systematic effort to elevate attitudes vis-a-vis woman from the misogynistic to the non-discriminatory, moving towards the ideal of "emptiness" (an absence of differences) to universal salvation.

It is important to view such rationalizations in their specific religious context. Buddhist texts were written by men for men committed to a non-sensual goal in life. This being the case, they reveal a sharp instinct for self-preservation. That their view of woman was misogynistic comes as no surprise. The attribution of seductive powers to woman was indicative of the perceived potential threat to monastic spiritual welfare, not necessarily to organizational leadership or administrative superiority. Cast in the role of evil temptress, woman represented daughters incarnate of Mara, the god of evil — namely, Lust, Avariciousness, and Craving — who could easily lead astray frail human beings unable to achieve the desire-less state essential to Buddhism. The evil power of sexuality associated with woman intensified monastic insecurity since sexual desire was the greatest of evils that caused endless rebirth and cyclical pain. That woman was a pollutant whose contaminating effect was to be avoided has been recorded in Buddha's warnings to his disciple Ananda, i.e., If confronted by woman — men should not look, listen nor talk, but otherwise keep wide awake. In addition to being a cause of mental anguish and pain, woman was considered a competitor in the monastic community as well as a danger to family stability on account of their aspirations for nunhood and adulterous behavior.

Outside the religious domain, Buddhist monks were less defensive in their assessment of woman. As mother, she was viewed with compassion owing to the intrinsic pain of attachment to the world of children which prevented her active involvement in non-domestic endeavors. Nevertheless, the paragon of womanhood was still the bearer of sons whose most exalted function was the regeneration of society. As good daughter and friend, woman's unquestioning dependence and subordination in the conduct of day to day affairs was accorded an aura of religiosity as in the exercise of the Hindu Dharma or duty. However, when woman dared to venture on to the religious path, great concern was expressed regarding their failure to discharge the important responsibility of ensuring family continuity and social stability. In any case, woman as nun was to be subordinated even to the youngest of monks to preserve the hierarchical order of a patriarchal society.

On the matter of ultimate salvation, Buddhist sutras prescribed rebirth as a man. This was a necessary condition for entry into the bodhisattva path or sainthood not unlike the Hindu tenet imposing rebirth as a Brahman as a prerequisite for Moksa or release from cyclical existence. The implied sexual change was ambivalently seen either as a physiological process involving mental sexual power to control physical changes or a symbolic process of mental transition from sensual existence to a state of desirelessness or Nirvana. However, notions of sexuality, male or female, were viewed as mental attachments and distinctions that contradicted the Buddhist ideal of Emptiness and Asexuality. Thus in the idealized conceptions of the Buddha in a state of spiritual perfection, there has been a deliberate concealment of the sexual organ, representing perhaps a symbolic neutralization of sexual desire or negation of sexual energy through meditation.

Definitely, Buddhist literature is replete with contradictory claims regarding egalitarianism and sexual competitiveness. The prejudiced mind was one to be eventually enlightened but often failed. This situation is vividly capsulized in a terse Buddhist anecdote: One day, the monk Tanzen carried a woman across the river upon the vehement objection of a fellow religious named Ekido, who reminded him of the rule against associating with women. To this, the wise monk Tanzen replied — "I carried and left her on the river bank... are you still carrying her in your mind?"

Protectionist Prescriptions and Practices

An enduring socio-cultural system that has successfully institutionalized its basic beliefs in the wake of political, economic and technological developments, Islam continues to exercise pervasive influence on the role and status of woman, apparently overshadowing Buddhism or even Hinduism. Although it presently encompasses a regional population of close to 800 million believers in different stages of modernization, the general impression has remained strong that under Islam, woman's subjugation under man is condoned. The elaborate system of religious laws and injunctions originating from the Koran as interpreted by male lawyers and theologians allows the continuous transmission and adaptation of commands and norms to suit existing and changing social conditions. Thus it is in the pages of Muslim living tradition that one finds convincing arguments as to why Asian woman must perforce continue to struggle if only to change an image borne out of centuries of subjugation.

As in Hindu and Buddhist tradition, sexual powers have always been highly valued in Islam. Sexuality is a positive factor necessary for Muslim community regeneration. Viewed in a religious light, sexual satisfaction gives man a preview of the delights of Paradise. This makes sex an incentive to pursue perfection, fulfilling God's will while gratifying one's self.

With regards to female sexuality in particular, Koranic interpretation is said to characterize woman as an active rather than as a passive sexual being. As such, woman is a powerful and dangerous force with an ability to deceive and defeat man not through physical strength but by cunning and intrigue. The term "fitna" or chaos (which in Moroccan means beautiful woman) is used to describe the condition of man distracted from his social and religious duties by woman. In this context, the overwhelming attractiveness of woman which erodes man's resistance is considered the most destructive element in the Muslim social order.

On the strength of this observation, Muslim society has thus seen it fit that woman be controlled so as not to tempt man. From this has arisen various rules governing spatial segregation and limitations on modes of social interaction. To protect society, i.e., men, prescriptions to foster male dominance, at the same time curb female sexuality, were put in place. This is exemplified by notions of the eminence of man over woman. Rules to regulate woman's life were codified into a family law. For example, it is considered the duty of man to provide for the material and physical needs of his wife. Woman can be repudiated unilaterally and, in an ensuing divorce, the husband retains custody of the children. Muslim men are allowed four wives. Relative to a man, a woman is entitled only to half an inheritance, in the same way that her testimony is worth only one half that of a man's.

Although these injunctions stemmed from the assumption of an active female sexuality that had to be bridled, Koranic reference to biological inferiority is also used against woman. Thus the privilege to assume high social and political positions such as the conduct of war in defense of Allah has been traditionally reserved for men.

Not to be overlooked are the variations in Islamic perspectives on male-female relations as defined by different subgroups within Islam such as those belonging to the so-called Traditionalists, Modernists, Secularists, and the Fundamentalists. However, suffice it to note that with the advent of modernization in Islamic societies, where man's social standing has been modified by westernized versions of the law, modes of employment, and styles of administration, one area of control has remained. In the family domain, man continues to assert his superior role in a conscious effort to curtail the sexual freedom and the ensuing susceptibility to marital infidelity of modernized Islamic woman.

In general, following Islamic Fundamentalist prescriptions, woman is to be loved. Although treated with compassion and consideration and respected as an equal, she is seen as different from man. Islam persists as a masculine religion which imposes spiritual duties only on men, with privileges of participation extended to women. In judicial matters, greater responsibility is assigned to man who is vested with a dominant position as reinforced by his right to inherit 50% more than woman and his continuing obligation and prerogative to provide for the family inspite of a working wife. For the same reason, men are fined 50% less for killing a woman, and to the same extent woman's testimony is devalued relative to that of a man. To preserve marital harmony, it is the man who must take final charge in conjugal affairs notwithstanding joint decision-making. Marriage requires mutual consent, although as a contract, it is a pact between male family members alone. Even with monogamy as the norm, divorce is a man's right under which woman is allowed to be taken back or eventually to remarry at his discretion. Like all conservative systems, requisite decency of dress and segregation of the sexes in school and in the workplace imply a protectionist attitude vis-a-vis woman. This is best exemplified in the continuing idealization of motherhood as the enviable state that spares woman from the struggles and hardships of a career and allows her to draw security from the family.

Images and Options

Hinduism, Buddhism and Islam have contributed in varying degrees to the curtailment of woman's social mobility in their respective spheres of influence in Asia. Through customs, rites and rituals associated with these traditional religions, Asian woman has been cast in a stereotype mold as weak and suppliant, submissive and subordinate. Left in the hands of male lawgivers, scholars and priests whose prolific writings go back to centuries, woman became an object of constancy rather than an agent of change. Within a self-perpetuating system characterized by male dominance in every field of worthy endeavor, there was no chance for redemption. To put it in a manner of speaking—her image was "shot"—which only goes to show the incalculable power of the written and spoken word!

And yet, in a sense, woman was afforded options within the Asian religious framework. That the majority accepted a pragmatic approach to instill a sense of order and harmony within the family and the larger social group is not to say that others failed to pick up the challenge to be different. However, it can be safely surmised that these were few and far between. For like the fabled Indian woman philospher Gorgy, they might have been admonished thus: "Gorgy, do not study too hard.. your head might fall off!" Is it any wonder then that inspite of the three religions' common perception of the inestimable seductive power of woman, no daughters incarnate of the evil Mara have been recorded as spearheading a subversive pro-female movement. To this very day, the work has yet to be done. Ⱄ

REFERENCES

Basham, A.L. *The Wonder that was India.* (Oxford University Press, 1960).

Muhammad, Abdul Rauf (ed). (New York: R Speller, 1979).

Paul, Diana. *The Buddhist Feminine Ideal.* (Missoula, Montreal: Scholars Press, 1980).

_____. *Women in Buddhism.* (Berkeley, California: Humanities Press. 1979).

Utas, Bo. *Women in Islamic Societies.* (London: Curzon Press, 1983).

REFLECTIONS ON WOMEN IN HINDU LITERATURE

Susan P. Evangelista

In India it is especially difficult to separate cultural practices from religious traditions because Hinduism actually encompasses both realms and is, in fact, a monolithic system, a way of life. The hard lot of women in India is well-known and this emerges in a variety of contexts. In our newspapers we read of bride-burning rituals, the outright murder of women whose dowries did not meet the expectations of the groom's family. In nutrition studies we see pictures of boy-girl twins, about two years old, and notice that the boy has perhaps twice the body weight of the girl because he is always fed first. Surely such practices as these do not have religious sanction.

On the other hand, the old practice of widow-burning did seem to have religious backing, if not explicitly, at least in the fact that the rules laid down for living widows in the *Artha-sastra* made life so difficult that even death might seem preferable. Also, the stereotype of the much-admired *proper* wife, Sita, who describes herself as the shadow of her lord's substance is laid down in the sacred epic *The Ramayana*.

But no generalization about India is fair. For every "truth" one can pick out of the holy scriptures, its contradiction can be found as well. If Sita is the much-admired, totally submissive wife of Rama, Draupadi, much more spirited and aggressive, is the wife of *all five* of the Pandu brothers, heroes of the equally-sacred *Mahabharata*. And if the wife of Lord Shiva sometimes appears as the beautiful, demure Parvati, she may also appear as the blood-thirsty black goddess Kali, with a string of men's heads around her neck and a girdle of severed arms dangling from her waist.

Kali, the Mother Goddess, is in fact very important in Hinduism and is the prime object of worship of millions of Hindus, especially among the Bengalis. A.L. Basham points out that Mother Goddesses have always been worshipped in India, even in pre-Hindu times. In Hinduism, they represent an incorporation of pre-Aryan influences but the incorporation has been made universally. The goddess, says Basham, is seen as "the *sakti*, the strength or potency of her male counterpart. It was thought that the god was inactive and transcendent, while his female element was active and immanent...."[1]

Heinrich Zimmer makes the same point with his quotation from Sri Ramakrishna:

> *The Primordial Power is ever at play. She is creating, preserving and destroying in play, as it were. This power is called Kali. Kali is verily Brahman, and Brahman is verily Kali. It is one and the same reality. When we think of It as inactive, that is to say not engaged in the acts of creation, preservation, and destruction, then we call It Brahman. But when It engages in these activities, then we call It Kali or Sakti. The reality is one and the same; the difference is in name and form.*[2]

So the female element here is part of the male, the potent and immanent part. And since Kali is associated with Lord Shiva, the God of Destruction (the destruction of the temporal being is, in Hinduism, a necessary step towards the realization of the absolute), Kali is wild-eyed, blood-thirsty and actually demands living sacrifices in her temples. Legend has it that Kali once killed a terrible demon from whose blood would spring a new demon if its drops would touch the ground. To prevent the blood from spilling to the ground, Kali drank it all, and thus developed her morbid taste.

If we consider that *The Mahabharata* is full of stories involving women and is eleven times as long as *The Iliad* and *The Odyssey* combined yet it is only a part of the Hindu sacred literature, it would seem unwise to even attempt to make a definitive statement about women in Hinduism. We may profit more if we look into the work of the Indian writer Rabrindranath Tagore, a Hindu gentleman and scholar, a Bengali and humanist. Tagore (1861-1941), widely recognized as one of the great thinkers of India, wrote a great deal of religious literature — plays with complicated religious themes and devotional poetry. His religious literature range from the problems of enlightenment, selfhood and self-respect, detachment in relation to compassion, the finite and the infinite, to more specific conflict situations, like the problem of blood-sacrifices in the temples of Kali, or the relationship between Hinduism and Buddhism, the heterodox religious movement in the same tradition. From these plays we can derive many insights into women's roles in religious experiences. In this literature we find no black-or-white polarities, but a complex spectrum of shades and hues of the religious possibilities of the female.

Tagore's *Sacrifices*, one of the best-known and most frequently anthologized plays, deals with the problem of the blood sacrifices being offered to Kali's temple and the rising conflict between the church and state, the priest and king, the Brahmin and the Kshyatria. The play opens with the queen praying to the capricious Kali, who apparently has not seen it fit to grant the queen a child. She promises Kali three hundred kids and one hundred buffalo as blood sacrifices. With neat parallelism, a young peasant girl named Aparna appears before King Govinda and Jaising, a Kshyatria boy who serves as adopted son and assistant to the temple priest. Aparna is poor but she has what the queen lacks — a child — the child of a goat, the creature the queen has promised to Kali. But Aparna's goat had already been captured and sacrificed to the Black Goddess — she saw his blood running down the temple steps, and had thus come to the king to beg, too late, for mercy.

But she does succeed in moving the king, who then proclaims that henceforth there shall be no blood sacrifices to Kali. This brings King Govinda into direct conflict with the priest Raghupati, who lives for the goddess alone, convinced that she preserves the order of the state and that she must have blood sacrifices. He accuses Govinda of usurping power that is not his, of interfering in the realm of religion which should rightfully be left to the Brahmin. Govinda however, turns the tables around by saying that the Goddess Kali appeared to him in the guise of the peasant girl Aparna and pleaded for compassion, saying that she no longer wants blood sacrifices.

From this point on much of the play is devoted to political intrigue, as the priest tries to undermine the king's power by having the people rally against him, by buying out his generals, by bribing his brother with the kingship, telling the man that Kali must have king's blood, if not Govinda's, then his own. Jaising, Raghupati's assistant, resists the notion that the Goddess would want brother to kill brother and finally offers his own *Kshyatria* (kingly) blood to Kali, killing himself at her altar. Jaising's death brings Raghupati to his senses, for he loved the young boy, and he too denies Kali and her blood thirst, casting the statue out of the temple. In the end he too follows the peasant girl Aparna, apparently seeing her as a more benevolent and compassionate Kali.

This is a powerful and intense play with tremendously strong characters, half of whom are women. Of the three women the queen is the only rather traditional one, wanting as she does a child above all. In fact her perceptions are filtered through this overpowering desire, so that she sees all actions, from the conflict between king and priest to the final destruction of Kali, solely in relation to her need for a child.

But the center of the play, the source of its power and intensity, is the Mother Goddess Kali, the black, immovable stone goddess. She is seen as whimsical and willful, giving no reason for her actions or for her bloodthirst. But the queen asks her to trade a blood sacrifice for fertility, the implication of which is that she controls the cycle of destruction and creation at will. She is the immanent, the doer, the power of the universe — and she is absolutely female, a mother, but without the usual traits of humility and self-sacrifice. She is not necessarily benevolent, but creation still rests on her.

Aparna, however, appears to be weak and suffering, but when she is seen as Kali, albeit Kali in a kinder form, she takes on great strength. She gives the king the courage to deny the priest, and she asks Jaising to transfer his devotion from the other Kali to her, and she eventually leads the priest away, for he too has accepted her as goddess. She carries with her the power of Kali, and even the potential for destruction. Creation now rests on her, though she is still the simple peasant girl. The men in this play are operating on the surface, going through utterly meaningless political struggles, while the women are in touch with the essential realities of the universe.

Malini is another play in which Kali and her cult of (male) worshippers is predominant. This time the conflict is between Hinduism and Buddhism. Malini is a king's daughter, but a Buddhist convert in a Hindu kingdom. The Brahmins are much alarmed at this threat to their religion (or perhaps to their religious authority), and they demand an audience with the king, telling him that "a snake has raised its poisonous food from his own nest, and is aiming at the heart of our sacred religion."[3] The priests therefore demand Malini's banishment.

But for Malini, the call for her banishment apparently brings her to enlightenment. She sees it not as a call to banishment, but as a call to *join* the rest of the world:

> *I have come down to my exile at your call... I always knew that your doors were open for me. The cry went from you for my banishment and I woke up, amidst the wealth and pleasure of the king's house... I am exiled from my home, so that I may make your house my own.*[4]

Simultaneously, the angry Brahmins have been calling on the Mother Goddess Kali, "whose wrath is the sole weapon of worshippers". When Malini enters the scene, they assume that *she* is Kali. Even when they find out that she is the king's daughter, they accept her *in her exile* as the savior of their religion. Perhaps this is a metaphor for the paradoxical relationship between Hinduism and Buddhism, in which Buddhism saves and revitalizes Hinduism by being itself cast out! And once again we see the source of life, salvation, destruction – in a word, the essential power of the universe – clearly centered on the female, in the Mother Goddess Kali, and by derivation in a more earthly young girl who had the strength and the openness of heart enough in touch with the essence to become Kali. (On the level of the essential in the Hindu-Buddhist framework, all beings are the same, and this accounts for the possibility of Kali revealing herself as Malini, or as Aparna.)

In *Natir Puja*, an extremely complex play on the relationship between Hinduism and Buddhism, There is again a young woman follower of the Buddha who suffers willingly for her convictions. Srimati is a low-caste girl, a humble palacedancer in a kingdom divided by religion. But as a devout Buddhist she has been given the honor of offering worship at the shrine of the Buddha on his birthday. This of course enrages the Buddhist princesses one of whom is especially jealous. When the princess found out who chose Srimati — the Bhikshus — she points out that these people had lower-caste origins. The Bhikshuni did not mind this, saying that in Buddhism they are all one.

But the ruling queen and prince are Hindu and the kingdom is divided, and thus the fact that Srimati will do worship to the Buddha means that she has willingly accepted the death of a religious martyr. Srimati has been warned but is self-possessed and serene as she announces that she has no fear to do worship at the Buddha's shrine. And while she might possibly be able to escape with an inconspicuous form of worship, she has chosen to pay her respects by dancing, determined to be true to her character and to offer the Buddha her best. We feel, even beyond her strength of character, the depth of her religious enlightenment and her contact with the essential world.

Nandini, heroine of the play *Red Oleanders*, is another deeply enlightened young woman, this time completely within the traditional Hindu scheme. There is no talk of God in this play. It takes place in a suffocating town from which there is no way out, where men are enslaved to mine gold, prodded by the greed of a king who himself is not free. The king lives behind iron nets, and until the very end appears only as a voice. It is a militarized state, with spies, goon squads and forced labor, with paranoia and suspicion among the workers. Nandini is, however, completely self-possessed (this is a general characteristic of the deeply enlightened, those who are in touch with the essence of the universe), wandering freely and cheerfully, rising above the restrictions, immune to the mistrust. There are certainly those who mistrust her and feel the threat that her character poses to the repressive system. Like any purely enlightened figure, she deeply affects all those with whom she comes into contact, reawakening in them their humanity and their free spirit. Says Bishu to her.

> *Ever since coming to Yaksha Town the sky has dropped out of my life. I felt as if they had pounded me in the same mortar with all the fractions of men here, and rolled us into a solid lump.*

> *Then you came and looked into my face in a way that made me sure some light could still be seen through me...*

> *Yes, you are my messenger from the unreachable shore. The day you came to Yaksha Town a gust of salt air knocked at my heart.*[5]

Nandini has charmed even the king ensnared in a prison of his own making, because she alone is unafraid of him. The play concludes with Nandini fearlessly giving her own life to liberate the workers and to topple the whole police state.

There is something particularly appealing about the female martyr, the female liberator. Although Tagore also uses parallel male characters in other plays, the female is somehow less rigid, more open to enlightened spontaneity. Neither Malini, Srimati nor Nandini experience inner conflict or self-division. They are purely and simply vehicles of God, vehicles of Kali. Their courage and their power over others both stem from this fact.

But Tagore's women are not *just* enlightened vehicles of God, they *can* experience conflicts and grow during the course of the play. In *Chitra*, Tagore enlarges an incident described in the *Mahabharata*, where Arjuna falls in love with the very masculine princess Chitra. Chitra has long been in love with Arjuna, but she was raised as a boy, since her father had no male heir. She was taught to hunt and shoot; thus she knew no feminine wiles for winning hearts. He hands were strong to bend the bow, but never learned Cupid's archery the play of eyes. [6]

She implores the god of love to make her beautiful for one day, so that she might win Arjuna's love and tempt him to break his vow of celibacy.

Chitra's wish is granted; she becomes beautiful, and Arjuna falls in love with her and in fact makes love to her. But the moment Chitra has what she thought she wanted, she becomes doubtful: the Chitra that Arjuna loves is not the real Chitra, but an enchanted version. Chitra goes back to the god of love and complains:

> Heaven came so close to my hand that I forgot for a moment that it had not reached me. But when I woke in the morning from my dream I found that my body had become my own rival. It is my hateful task to deck her everyday, to send her to my beloved, and see her caressed by him. Oh god, take back thy boon![7]

Chitra has discovered her selfhood and her self-respect, and she would deny any form of love that was false to this self. In chiding Arjuna for breaking his own vow, she says:

> O, shame upon you! What have you seen in me that makes you false to yourself? Whom do you seek in

*these dark eyes, in these milk-white arms, if you are
ready to pay for her the price of your probity? Not my
true self, I know. Surely this cannot be love, this is not
man's highest homage to woman. Alas, that this frail
disguise, the body, should make one blind to the light of
the deathless spirit!*[8]

Chitra sees that Arjuna's love for her is given at the
expense of her self-respect, and thus she rejects that kind of
love.

In another play, *Chandalika*, the conflict between the
values of sexual love and personal religious commitment sur-
faces with frightening intensity. In this short play, an untouchable girl, a chandalika named Prakriti meets Ananda,
the great disciple of the Buddha, at the well and Ananda asks
her for water. Within the context of the caste system this is
an appalling thing, for the girl is untouchable and the water is
therefore unclean. But the Buddhists reject caste, and by his
recognition of the personhood of Prakriti, Ananda gives her
self-recognition as well. He also inspires her love.

But the next time he sees her, he ignores her. This further ignites her passion -- a passion which seems to be for herself as well as for his love from which her self-hood must
spring. She forces her mother to use black magic on Ananda,
to drive him wild with desire so that he will come to her.
Eventually, he does come, but at the very moment that he
enters her presence, two things happen: Buddha, or perhaps
Ananda's own religious commitment, stops him, *and* the
Chandalika herself suddenly rejects her desire for him.

There is irony in the fact that the conflict is between
Ananda's religious commitment and the Chandalika's physical desire, and yet it is that very religious commitment which
created Prakriti's need for Ananda. Ananda asked her for
water, and taught her to recognize herself:

*Only once did he cup his hands, to take the water from
mine. Such a little water, yet that water grew to a
fathomless, boundless sea. In it flowed all the seven
seas in one, and my caste was drowned, and my birth
washed clean... I may truly call it my new birth! He
came to give me the honor of quenching Man's thirst...
My heart has been dancing ever since, and night and
day I hear those solemn tones – 'Give me water, give
me water.'*[9]

Up until the end, Prakriti continues to see Ananda's love (lust) for her as necessary for her own new self-hood. Looking into the magic mirror which shows her Ananda wherever he is, she says

> I beheld the God of Creation, more terrible far than the God of Destruction, lashing the flames to work His purposes, while they writhed and roared in anger... My mind swelled with a joy hard to name -- joy in the tremendous detachment of new creation... [10]

and later,

> No curse, it brings no curse, it brings the gift of my new birth. The thunderbolt hammers open the Lion-gates of death; the door breaks, the walls crumble, the falsehood of this birth of mine is shattered... My All-destroyer, my All-in-all, you have come!"

But at the very moment of Ananda's entrance, Prakriti seems to understand that she cannot gain her own dignity at Ananda's expense, for the magically-inspired lust for her has taken away *his* human dignity. And without *his* dignity, there would be no source for *hers*.

> Oh Mother, Mother, stop! Undo the spell now – at once— undo it! What have you done? What have you done? Oh wicked, wicked deed! — better have died. What a sight to see! Where is the light and radiance, the shining purity, the heavenly glow? How worn, how faded has he come to my door! Bearing his self's defeat as a heavy burden, he comes with drooping head... Away with all this, away with it! (She kicks the paraphernalia of magic to pieces.) Prakriti, Prakriti, if in truth you are no Chandalini, offer no insult to the heroic! Victory, victory to him. [12]

So the Chandalini, too, has discovered her own selfhood and a self-respect that is now independent of Ananda's love.

This play obliquely touches on another problem that is traditional in Indian literature, and that is the conflict between human compassion and religious liberation. The quest for liberation or *moksha* presumably removes a person from other human obligations, and sexual love surely belongs to the world of *maya*, illusion and impermanence which one wants to be liberated from. Yet at the same time, liberation should be *humanizing,* as it was for Nandini, who loved freely. There is the tradition of the cold, unfeeling ascetic, but religious depth may seem lacking in such a figure.

The following Zen story is not Indian, but it is Buddhist, and it may serve to illuminate the issue:

> There was an old woman in China who had supported a monk for over twenty years. She had built a little hut for him and fed him while he was meditating. Finally she wondered just what progress he had made in all this time.
>
> To find out, she obtained the help of a girl rich in desire. "Go and embrace him", she told her, "and then ask him suddenly, 'What now?'"
>
> The girl called upon the monk, and without much ado carressed him, asking him what he was going to do about it.
>
> "An old tree grows on a cold rock in winter," replied the monk somewhat poetically. "Nowhere is there any warmth."
>
> The girl returned and related what he had said.
>
> "To think I fed that fellow for twenty years!" exclaimed the old woman in anger. "He showed no consideration for your need, no disposition to explain your condition. He need not have responded to passion, but at least he should have evidenced some compassion."
>
> She at once went to the hut of the monk and burned it down.[13]

Tagore deals more explicitly with this problem in his short play *Sanyasi*. A *sanyasi* is a holy man, one whose life is given over to his quest for liberation, and when this play opens, the *sanyasi* speaks of how he has stilled even the flow of night and day in his mind, meditating in a dark cave in which he knew neither time nor season. But there he is out in the village, and we hear with him the emptiness, the foolish boastfulness, the argumentativeness of the people around him. A woman raises her voice at a poor untouchable girl. Raghu's daughter, because she fears that the child has

touched and thus polluted her. The child then approaches
the *sanyasi:*

Vasanti:	*I am Vasanti, Raghu's daughter. May I come to you, father?*
Sanyasi:	*Why not, child?*
Vasanti:	*I am a pollution, as they call me.*
Sanyasi:	*But they are all that – a pollution.*
	They roll in the dust of existence. Only he is pure who has washed away the world from his mind...
Vasanti:	*Will you touch me?*
Sanyasi:	*Yes, because nothing can touch me truly.*[14]

The *sanyasi's* answer is enlightened, worthy of Nandini, who
can combine compassion and detachment, who can be res-
ponsive and yet untouched. Yet later in the play the *sanyasi*
begins to feel suffocated by the little girl's love, and feels
himself slipping back into the ways of the world:

> *What game of yours is this with me, little girl? I am a Sanyasi, I have cut all my knots, I am free... But where was hidden in my heart this snake, this anger, that hissed out of the dark with its fang? No, they are not dead – they outline starvation. These hell creatures clatter their skeletons and dance in my heart....*[5]

So he returns to his cave, to attempt to rid himself once more
of his human feelings, leaving the girl sobbing behind him.
Sometime later he once again comes out of his cave, but this
time the human conversations he hears around him have a
sense of warmth and togetherness, and thus he decides that
liberation must be *in* the world instead of away from it:

> *Let my vows of sanyasi go. I break my staff and my alms bowl. This stately ship, this world, which is crossing the sea of time – let it take me up again, let me join once more the pilgrims. Oh, the fool who wanted to seek safety in swimming alone, and gave up the light of the sun and stars, to pick his way with his glow-worm's lamp!... I am free among things and forms and purpose. The finite is the true infinite, and love knows its truth. My girl, you are the spirit of all that is —I can never leave you.*[16]

He goes back to the village only to be told that the girl is
dead. But still thinking of her as "the true infinite", "the

spirit of all that is", he ends the play by saying that she can never die.

It seems then that the answer to the problem of religious detachment versus compassion is just that: the true infinite is found in the finite, and the finite, as we have seen, is the manifest, the immanent, the *sakti*, the female side of divinity.

The Hindus realized this, and Tagore obviously saw it clearly, but the Buddhists institutionalized it by way of the Bodhisattvas, those compassionate beings who delayed their own salvation to help the rest of the world. The Indian Bodhisattva Avalokitesvara, the most compassionate of all, could indeed hear the infinite in the finite cries of the world. It would seem to me no accident that by the time this Bodhisattva had made his way to China, he had evolved into the female Kwan Yin. ⊗

ENDNOTES

[1]A.L. Basham, *The Wonder that was India*. (Fontana Ancient History 1967.), p. 313.

[2]Heinrich Zimmer, *Philosophies of India*. (Cleveland: The World Publishing Co., 1956.), p. 564.

[3]*Collected Poem and Plays of Rabindranath Tagore*. (MacMilla: London, 1967.), p. 486.

[4]Ibid., p. 488.

[5]Rabindranath Tagore, *Red Oleanders*. (Madras: The Macmillan Co. of India, 1979, First Edition 1925.), pp. 38-9.

[6]*Collected Poems and Plays....* p. 154.

[7]Ibid., p. 162-3.

[8]Ibid., p. 159.

[9]Rabindranath Tagore, *Three Plays: Mukha-dhara, Natir Puja, Chandalika*. Translated by Marjorie Sykes. (Oxford University Press: London, 1950.) p. 138-9.

[10]Ibid., p. 150.

[11]Ibid., p. 152.

[12]Ibid., 153-4.

[13]Paul Reps, *Zen Flesh, Zen Bones*. A Doubleday Anchor Book. Garden City, New York), p. 10.

[14]*Collected Poems and Plays...* p. 468.

[15]Ibid., 472-3.

[16]Ibid., 477-8.

WOMEN IN BIBLICAL PATRIARCHY

Arche Ligo

The Bible is rooted in a patriarchal society, the Israelitic society of 1000-200 B.C. Together with parts of the New Testament, it is often taken to be the cause of women's inferior position in Christianized societies. There are, however, passages that uplift women's position and speak of women's roles to which we are unaccustomed today. But these messages of faith and liberation are couched in images and symbols of patriarchal culture. Thus, distinctions must be made between that culture and the message of the Book to provide a just account of women in Biblical patriarchy.

Women were almost always subordinate creatures in Hebrew Israelitic society. They were first under the control of their father, and then passed on to their husbands in marriage, and when they became widows, they were dependent on their sons. And woe unto her who had no son in her old age. It was through men that women gained access to the economic resources of the community, as clearly demonstrated in the story of the rich woman of Shunem and the prophet Elisha (2 Kings 4:8-37). She would stand to lose everything if she lost her son. Widows without male supports fell into dire straits, as with Naomi in the Book of Ruth.

In fact, women were listed with the rest of the husband's property in the Ten Commandments (Ex 20:17). Children, too, were at their father's disposal, especially daughters (Ex 21:7). Startling stories of sexual disposal of women by their fathers or lovers are found in the story of Lot and his two daughters (Gen 19:4-8) and in the story of the Levite and his concubine (Judges 19:22-29).

Women could not inherit property in Israel. "A daughter could inherit from her father only if there were no son (Num 27:1-11), but she had to marry within the class so the property would not move out of it (Num 36:1-9). Women simply served as blood links to pass property from male to male within the family line."[1] She was always dependent on a man for her support.

Sexual transgressions of women were heavily punished. Adultery by woman "ranked with murder as a major crime and demanded the death penalty"[2] and she was either burned or stoned to death. These transgressions were serious crimes not because the woman was partner to sin but because the husband's property right had been violated. A man's infidelity was not a crime, unless the woman involved was herself married or bethroted to another.

Since the woman was a man's possession, he could dispossess, that is, divorce the woman, but she could not divorce him. All he needed to do was deliver a bill of divorce to his wife before two witnesses. In rabbinic writings it was considered obligatory to divorce a "bad wife" (Sirach 25:23-26).

The discrimination against women was not only economic and social but also religious. The rite of membership into the Israelitic religious community was circumcision (Gen 17:10ff) which excluded women. In the Temple, the women were confined in the Court of Women, which was nineteen steps higher than the Court of Gentiles but fifteen steps lower the Court of Israel. Only Israeli men were admitted in the Court of Israel. Women who were within seven days after the end of their menstruation were denied entry to the temple, as were mothers within forty days following the birth of a boy or eighty days following the birth of a girl.

Given this patriarchal setting, whatever positive biblical statements there are about women come out all the more powerful. Let us examine Genesis 1 and 2. Both are creation stories, with Genesis 2 as an earlier story written around 1000 B.C. by Yahwist writer(s). Genesis 1 is a later account written around 500 B.C. by a Priestly writer.[3] Genesis 1 had an egalitarian description of creation. "God is described as creating humanity immediately in its dual sexual form; there is no priority or inferiority expressed or implied."[4] It is also important to note that the word used for "man" in Gen 1:26-27, ha adam, is a generic Hebrew term for humanity. It is not a proper name nor does it refer to man in the male sense.

Genesis 2 had been interpreted as reflecting man's superiority over woman because he was created first. This interpretation does not reflect the text's original meaning. The

Yahwist writer of Genesis 2 does not speak of prior creation of male humanity, undifferentiated. Yahweh God fashioned humanity (*ha adam*) from the dust of the earth (*ha adamah*). Here the Yahwist writer indulges in a play of words: *ha adam* taken from *ha adamah* (feminine). In verses 18-20, the writer expresses the idea that it is not good for humanity to be singular; that to be fully human, there must be relationships, dialogue between two equals. All the way to verse 23, the author uses the term *ha adam*, then, in the same verse he refers to women as *ishshah* taken out of an *ish*. "The writer's main intent would seem to be that the word wo-man (*ishshah*) is taken from the word man (*ish*) the word *ishshah* appears... basically to be the word *ish* with the feminine suffix *ah* added to it."[5] But if confusion arises, the unwarranted conclusion at hand would be that woman was formed from the rib of man rather than from undifferentiated humanity.[6]

Phyllis Trible has a provocative analysis which deals with the parallel between *ish/ishshah* and *ha adam/ha adamah*.[7] She maintains that *ha adam* is not portrayed as inferior to the earth as he is, in fact, given power and authority over the earth. So humanity, taken from the earth, becomes superior to it. Applying this logic, *ishshah* (woman), being taken from *ish* (man), is superior to him. But that is not the meaning of Genesis 2:23. The context of the passage is in the preceding line "bone of my bone, and flesh from my flesh". It does not point to the woman's superiority but to the relationship of a couple in mutuality and equality. "Finally, woman is not derived from man, even as the earth creature is not derived from the earth. For both of them, life originates with God. Dust of the earth and rib of the earth creature are but raw materials for God's creative activity. Truly, neither woman nor man is an autonomous creature; birth owes their origin to divine mystery."[8]

If there is subordination of women now, it is understood by Genesis as a result of disobedience that set nature in disarray; animals and plants are no longer docile to man, woman's childbirth is no longer under her complete control, woman and man are no longer partners but dominant-subordinate to one another—all because the anchor of order was destroyed through humanity's disobedience.

Let us now turn to another story of women found in Judges 5, the story of Deborah and Jael. Judges 4 precedes it as a prose narrative, while chapter 5 is a triumphant ode or a battle song. Chapter 5 is an older text than chapter 4 and scholars agree that it might even be contemporaneous to the event. As a battle song Judges 5 has the following structure:9

Verses 1 - 5	Overture
	Subject (v2)
	Audience (v3a)
	Proclamation (v3b)
	Divine Intervention (vv4-5)
Verses 6 - 8	State of Israel Before the Deliverance
Verses 9 - 11	Repetition of Overture
	Subject (v9)
	Audience (v10)
	Proclamation (v11a)
	Divine Intervention (v11b)
Verses 12 - 18	Master of the Tribes
Verses 19 - 22	Actual Battle of Victory
Verses 23 - 30	Death of Sisera
	Reality (vv25-27) contrasted to
	Possibility (28-30)
Verse 31	Concluding Theology

Let us focus on chapter 5:3 where Deborah is spoken of as "mother in Israel." The events in the song fall into place when it answered the question "What does it mean to call Deborah a mother in Israel?" Her achievement described in chapter 4-5 were those of prophet, judge, military leader, singer and poet, talents which she used in order to deliver Israel from the hands of the enemies—the Canaanites led by Sisera.

"A mother in Israel then is one who brings liberation from oppression, provides protection, and ensures well-being and security for her people."10

An important thing to stress here is the context in which Deborah, a mother in Israel, emerged. Her presence as military leader and hero among the biblical cast of male leaders and heroes calls attention by contrast to the more usual position of women in patriarchal societies. Her story is a critique to patriarchal structures that blocked independence and leadership of women. At the same time we learn to appreciate the strength of those women in the Old Testament who appear in stereotyped roles, acting behind the scenes, ensuring the welfare and fortune of their people.

In conclusion to Deborah's story, the story of Jael is found. Jael, a Kenite, was the wife of Heber. They were nomadic tent-dwellers who lived in peaceful coexistence (Jvd 4:17). This fact makes Jael's killing of Sisera heinous and unlikely. Swidler in his book *Biblical Affirmation of Woman* interprets Jael's act as repugnant, deceitful, cowardly and unethical because it breached the code of hospitality central and important among nomadic tribes."

Socio-historical criticism of chapters 4 and 5 of Judges brings to light another perspective. It shows the underlying structure of the narrative and brings to the fore the unexpected power of women over men—that of Deborah and Jael over Barak and Sisera. "The fundamental interest of the story is to dramatize how Yahweh has given Israel power over Canaanite warriors through women rather than through men."[12]

Another contribution of socio-historical criticism is a social revolt theory that sees the emergence of the Israelite nation in Canaan as a result of neither military conquest or peaceful immigration. Instead, Israel emerged as a nation in a militant victory that arose from a long-brewing social revolt among depressed marginated Canaanite, restive peasant, pastoral nomad, *apirn*,[13] and other disaffected elements. The Exodus-Israelites with their militant delivering Yahweh simply clinched the revolt by acting as a final catalyst.

Seen from this angle, Jael's nation could be an ally to Israel's struggle. Jael and her husband would belong to this group, called allies by N. Gottwald[14] which supported Israel while maintaining a separate status within the Israelite movement.[15] Jael's killing of Sisera thus becomes a revolutionary act and the praise of Jael in Judges 5:24-27 is understandable in this context.

Aftermath: The New Testament

The New Testament exhibits a shift in the attitude towards women. The shift was brought about largely by Jesus own pro-woman stance as he did his best to dismantle the rigid patriarchal system of his time (cf. Matt 10:37-39 and Luke 14:26). The Hellenistic culture where Christianity took root and spread also provided for a relatively liberal and high status for women. Women had extensive economic rights— they could buy, own and sell property and goods, and will them to others. In fact, there are wealthy women in Hellenistic times. Women were also present at social gatherings (symposia), participated in sports like the Olympics, pursued professions in medicine, science, literature and philosophy. Though Hellenistic state religions were restrictive of women, the burgeoning of eastern cults and mystery religions changed the situation for them. Women took part in these religious cults, they even led the rituals and performed the priestly roles, as for example in the Eleusian, Dionysian and Andanian mysteries.

This is the proper cultural context for majority of the Pauline anti-woman corpus in the New Testament. Paul's preoccupation in maintaining social order and social distinctions between men and women was a reaction against Hellenizing influences that tended to blur many of the traditional social distinctions and roles. It was not originally intended to dominate women. But in second and third generation Christianity, more and more patriarchal structures and male roles spread, suppressing women's roles and dislodging women's structures.

Examples of this are the New Testament injunctions called *Haufstafel* or household codes.[16] They must be understood within the context of 1 Peter 2:11-5:11. Mary Schertz observes that this text is organized in a "chiasm" or ring composition as follows.[17]

2:13-17	General injunction to the community to be subject to human authority
2:18-20	Specific injunction to slaves to be subject to their masters
2:21-24	Christological hymn which establishes the model of Christ's submission
3:1-6	Specific injunction to wives to submit to their husbands
3:8-22	General injunction to all not to return evil for evil

A symmetry is developed by this juxtaposition of a general injunction, a specific injunction, the hymn, a specific injunction, and a general injunction. This gives the text a deep unity which has 1 Peter 2:23 as its core expression: "He was insulted and did not retaliate with insults; when he was tortured he made no threats but he put his trust in the righteous judge."

The specific injunctions to slaves and wives, telling them to be subject even to unjust masters and un-Christian husbands, are rooted in the example of Jesus Christ who did not return an insult for an insult nor a threat to suffering. "These actions of not-repaying-in-kind, in the case of Christ as in the case of slaves and wives, are rendered meaningful by the appeal to a higher order, by yielding present injustice to the one who judges justly... an act accomplished precisely by not returning in kind. In this sense, submission to every human creation is an act performed by those who are free with respect to these human institutions because they are... slaves of God (2:16) and daughters of Sarah (3:6)."[18]

Both slaves and wives, therefore, imitate Christ, but they are Christ-like in deeds as well as sufferings. The mention of bad masters and un-Christian husbands displays awareness that slavery and patriarchy are not divine institutions but human ones which cause problems for the community. The ethic of "returning good for evil" thus implies a critique of slavery and patriarchy. Submission, consequently, is framed in a wider discourse in which women are urged to advance freedom in the world through a revolutionary charity drawn from their own strength as women. ஃ

ENDNOTES

[1]Swidler, Leonard. *Biblical Affirmations of Woman.* (Philadelphia: The Westminster Press, 1966), p. 141.

[2]Coyle, Kathleen. *"Women in Church Tradition"* in *Religious Studies Vol. VIII.* Ed. Erlinda Bragado and Amador Bala. (Manila: DLSU), p. 2.

[3]Bible scholars basically agree that the work of at least five writers can be gleaned in the books of Genesis, Exodus, Leviticus, Numbers and Deuteronomy. They are the Yahwist or J, 10th century BC; the Elohist or E, 9th century B.C.; the Deuteronomist or D, 7th-6th century B.C.; and the Priestly or P, 5th century B.C.

[4]Swidler, p. 75.

[5]Ibid., p. 77.

[6]Genesis 2:18-24 should read:
Yahweh God said. "It is not good for humanity (*ha adam*) to live alone (*lebadda*) I will prepare for it a partner (*ezer neged*)." So from the soil Yahweh God fashioned all the wild beasts and all the birds of heaven. These he brought to humanity (*ha adam*) to see what it would call them; each one was to bear the name humanity (*ha adam*) would give it. Humanity (*ha adam*) gave names to all cattle, all the birds of heaven and all the wild beasts. But no partner (*ezer neged*) suitable for humanity (*ha adam*) was found for it. So Yahweh God made humanity (*ha adam*) fall into a deep sleep.. Yahweh God built the rib he had taken from humanity (*ha adam*) into a women (*ishshah*) and presented her to humanity (*ha adam*). Humanity (*ha adam*) exclaimed:

"This at last is bone from my bones,
and flesh from my flesh!
This is to be called wo-man (*ishshah*),
for this was taken from man (*ish*).
    This is why a man (*ish*) leaves his father and mother and joins himself to his wife, and they became one body."
    The Word for partner or companion is used here is the Hebrew *ezer* which does not imply inferiority, as can be seen in Pss 33:20; 115:9-11; 124:&; 145:5-6; Ex 18:4 and Dt 33:78,26, 29 where God is an ezer to humanity. Furthermore, the word *neged* adjoining *ezer* indicates equality, meaning literally "alongside of".

[7]Trible, Phyllis, *God and the Rhetoric of Sexuality*, (Philadelphia: Fortress Press, 1978), pp. 100f.

[8]Ibid.

[9]Jerome Biblical commentory, 8:19-21, p. 154

[10]Exum, J. Cheryl. "Mother in Israel" in *Feminist Interpretation of th Bible*, ed. Letty Russel, (Philadelphia: Westminster Press, 1985) p. 85.

[11]Swidler, p. 111-112.

[12]Gotwald, Norman. *The Hebrew Bible, A Socio-literary Introduction*. (Philadelphia: Fortress Press, 1985), pp. 253-254.

[13]Apirn are social outsiders turned to robbery or mercenary service, which gave them leverage in the infighting among city-state, sometimes they retreated to mountain redoubts.

[14]Gotwald, p. 272-276.

[15]Ibid, p. 274.

[16]Schroeder, David. "The New Testament Haustafel: Egalitarian or Status Quo?" in *Perspectives on Feminist Hermeneutics*, No. 10, Ed. Gayle Gerber Koontz and Willard Swartley. (Elkhart: Institute of Mennonite Studies, 1987), p. 56-64.

    Examples of *Haufstafel* include 1 Peter 3:17, Ephesians 5:21-33, Colossians 3:18-25, Titus 2:13-19.

[17]Schertz, Mary. "Likewise you wives... Another look at 1 Peter 2:11-5:11 in *Perspective on Feminist Hermenetics, #*10 ... p. 77.

    A ring composition or a chiasm is a literary construction in which the first line or element of a composition is similar to the last line or element; the second line or element similar to the second from the end; the third similar to the third from the end, etc. This construction is a device used for emphasis.

[18]Schertz, p. 80.

EMPOWERMENT OF WOMEN FOR PEACE*

Sr. Helen Graham, MM

To speak of the empowerment of women for peace from the perspective of the biblical traditions requires that we enter the world of the Bible to understand its peace sentiments and to appreciate the role played by women in the biblical period. In this paper, I hope to inquire first into the meaning of the biblical *shalom*, and into the concepts of power and empowerment, and then to attempt to understand how selected women from the Bible functioned within the constraints of the patriarchal environment that characterized biblical society. Lastly, I shall attempt to outline how Christian women (particularly Christian women of Asia) might be empowered to engage in the urgent evangelical task of building structures of peace within a world increasingly characterized by violence.

The Meaning of Biblical Shalom

To inquire into the meaning of the biblical *shalom* requires that we go beyond the dictionary meaning. This is necessary because words function as meaningful entities only within the framework of a sentence. There are approximately 350 occurences of *shalom* and its derivatives to be found within the Hebrew Bible and 85 occurences of the Greek *eirene* in the Christian scriptures.

A large number of biblical passages present the reader with a rather straightforward occurence of *shalom* where the meaning is easily discerned. For example, when Qohelet (or Ecclesiastes) places the word *shalom* in direct antithesis to the Hebrew word for war in Eccles 3:8, it is clear that *shalom* here means peace as the opposite of war. Likewise, when it is said in the Book of Judges that Sisera, the commanding gene-

---

*A talk prepared for the East Asia Area-World Federation of Methodist Women Seminar, Baguio City, April 11-15, 1988.

ral of King Jabin of Hazor's army, took refuge in the tent of Heber the Kenite because "there was *shalom* between Jabin... and the household of Heber the Kenite" (4:17), we understand that a relationship existed between the two households such that Sisera could expect protection.

But there are other places in the Hebrew Bible where the meaning of shalom is not at all so clear. When we read, for example, in Psalm 85 that,

> *Kindness and fidelity will meet,*
> *justice and* shalom *will embrace,*
> *Fidelity shall sprout from the earth ,*
> *and justice lean down from heaven (vs 13).*

we are at a loss as to the meaning of *shalom*. Similarly, when the great prophet of the exile says,

> *Then right will settle in the wilderness,*
> *and justice will inhabit the orchard,*
> *and the fruit of justice will be* shalom,
> *and the yield of justice quiet security forever*
> *(Isa 32:6-17)*

how are we to understand the meaning of *shalom?*

In these last two examples, we are dealing with poetry. Poetry thrives on the fact that words are open to multiple meaning. Poetic language, as Philip Wheelwright has said, "partly creates and partly discloses certain hitherto unknown, unguessed aspects of What Is". It is the aim of ordinary language to improve communication by limiting or reducing ambiguity, but speech that employs metaphor, such as poetry, has the extraordinary power of redescribing reality. In the words of the French philosopher, Paul Riceour, "Metaphor not only shatters the previous structures of our language, but also the previous structures of what we call reality".[1] It is, therefore, to the metaphorical occurences of *shalom* that we must look for empowerment in the task of building down structures of violence and building up structures of peace in today's world.

For the prophet Jeremiah, the preaching of those who fail to take into account the reality of impending destruction, and its social causes, is equivalent to attempting to heal a grevious wound with inadequate medication:

They have healed the wound of my people lightly.
saying, "Peace, peace" when there is no peace

(Jer 6:14: cf. 8:11).

One would have to study the sociohistorical context of the prophetic period of Jeremiah to appreciate fully what the "wound" of his people was. But whatever the wound was, the prophet asserts that it is bad medical practice to simply keep treating symptoms, to heal superficially; and it is bad social practice as well.

In the concluding exhortation of the section of the Book of Leviticus commonly referred to as the Holiness Code (chaps 17 to 26), *shalom* is described as a material blessing bestowed on the land by Yahweh. The passage reads:

> *If you walk in my statutes and observe my command-*
> *ments and do them, then I will give you your rains in*
> *their season, so that the land shall yield its increase,*
> *and the trees of the field shall yield their fruit. And*
> *your threshing shall last to the time of vintage, and the*
> *vintage shall last to the time for sowing; and you shall*
> *eat your bread to the full, and dwell in your land*
> *securely. Then I will give peace* (shalom) *in the land,*
> *and you shall lie down, and none shall make you*
> *afraid; and I will remove evil beasts from the land, and*
> *the sword shall not go through your land (Lev 26:3-6).*

For an agrarian people, the highest value is agrarian and biological productivity. Biblical Israel was an agrarian society. The theology represented in this passage from the Book of Leviticus is what might be termed an "if . . . then" theology. In return for walking in God's statutes and observing his commandments, God promises to supply the seasonal rains "so that the land shall yield its increase, and the trees of the field shall yield their fruit." The promised harvest will be of such bounty as to leave no interval between the grain threshing and vintage time, and between vintage time and the winter sowing. Abundance of food is here correlated with living securely in the land. Only then will Yahweh bestow the blessing of *shalom* in the land so that its inhabitants can sleep securely without fear of attack either from wild beasts or the sword of war. Biblical Israel's concept of *shalom* was concrete.

A similar juxtaposing of themes appears in a passage whose origin would seem to be toward the end of the period of the Babylonian exile. It is the Isaian version of this passage that is more familiar to us, but the Micah version is more complete. The passage reads:

This shall happen in the latter days:

The mount of the house of Yahweh
  will be established higher than the mountains;
it shall rise high above the hills.

Then peoples shall stream to it,
  and many nations will come and say:

"Come, let us go up to the mount of Yahweh,
to the house of the God of Jacob,
that he may teach us his ways,
that we may walk in his paths."

for out of Zion shall come instruction
and the word of Yahweh from Jerusalem.

He shall decide disputes between many peoples,
  and arbitrate for mighty and distant nations.
They will beat their swords into plough shares,
  and their spears into pruning-hooks.
One nation will not lift the sword against another,
  neither shall they learn war anymore.
Each one shall sit under their own vine
  and under their own fig tree,
  with none to terrify.

For the mouth of Yahweh of hosts has spoken.

(Micah 4:1-4; cf. Isa 2:2-4; translated by the author)

The passage makes the claim that when powerful nations from afar, who have been walking in their own way for too long, are converted and come seeking Yahweh's torah and Yahweh's way, then arms will be turned into implements for agrarian productions. The result will be security *(shalom)* as each one sits under their own vine and fig tree unafraid. The themes of obedience, agricultural productivity and the absence of the sword of war converge in this passage.

Many more passages could be cited, but these are perhaps sufficient to demonstrate that walking in Yahweh's statutes, observing his commandments and doing them, is what makes for *shalom*, i.e., is what brings down Yahweh's blessing upon the land in the form of agricultural bounty and security against wild beast and the sword of war. And if we ask what is meant by walking in Yahweh's statutes and observing his commandments to do them, the three major legal collections of the Pentateuch yield a rich harvest of social legislation demonstrating Yahweh's bias toward the poor, oppressed, marginated and exploited of the earth.[2] It is the observance of these commandments that brings the blessing of *shalom* upon the land.

But the opposite is also true. The failture to observe the social legislation meant to protect the vulnerable (symbolized in the Bible by the vulnerable trio: the widow, the fatherless and the stranger), would bring a curse upon the land in the form of the triple threat of famine, pestilence and the sword. It was this other side of the coin of the "if . . . then" theology that led Israel's prophets to the conviction that Yahweh had decreed destruction for the rulers of Samaria and Jerusalem.[3]

Biblical *shalom*, therefore, is a richer and more meaningful concept than that reflected by the English word "peace," which translates the Latin *pax*. The oldest meaning of *pax* is absence of war based on binding agreements between two parties to a conflict. It is essentially a negative concept, which while rejecting direct violence (i.e., war), does not address the structural conditions that constitute structural violence. It may even foster structural violence.[4] Our survey of biblical *shalom*, on the other hand, has shown us the positive meaning of peace as wholeness, completeness, fullness, health and prosperity, and the structures necessary to promote this condition. All too often, "peace" is associated with the maintainance of the status quo by those who benefit from the existing structure; i.e., those with the position and resources to maintain the inequitable structures of peacelessness characteristic of our contemporary 'civilization'. Empowerment of women for peace, therefore, implies directing women's peace efforts toward the realization of positive peace as represented by the biblical *shalom*.

Power and Empowerment

Before turning to selected passages dealing with women of the biblical period in relation to *shalom*, it might also be helpful if we take time to examine the concepts of power and empowerment.

Power is not a property or an attribute, but rather a relation. It requires a power-sender and power-receiver. There must be one who, by virtue of position and/or resources, is able to exercise effective power over another. "Power could be normative, based on persuasion; be remunerative, based on bargaining; or be punitive, based on force."[5] For persuasion to work, some degree of submissiveness is necessary; for bargaining to work, some kind of dependence; and for force to work, there must be an element of fear.[6]

Empowerment, therefore, would involve the capacity to counter this power-over-others with a countervailing power, power-over-self or autonomy. Through the building up of self-respect, self-sufficiency, and fearlessness one inoculates oneself against power-over-others from outside; one refuses to be a power-receiver.[7]

Power-over-others is operative in the vertical interaction relations of racism, sexism, classism, ageism, imperialism and environmental degradation. One party to the interaction is in a relationship of dominance with regard to the other, perceiving self as superior, and even as having a mandate to rule over the other. This interaction is essentially violent. But the violence is not overtly visible since it lies in the structure of interaction between the two social actors. It is only when the actor on the underside of the violent interaction becomes aware of the situation and begins to struggle against it, that a more direct form of violence makes its appearance in the form of force and repression. Empowerment for peace requires first an awareness or consciousness of the violent nature of this type of interactions based on equity. Such consciousness and commitment cannot but involve struggle.

As women become aware of, and are empowerd to counter, one or other of these manifestations of structural violence, they are actually involved in efforts to build *shalom* which, in its biblical understanding, is essentially well-being on *all* levels of society. For sexism, racism, ageism, clericalism, militarism, imperialism and environmental degredation are all aspects of peacelessness or lack of well-being.

Various women's movements in the Third World, spontaneous as well as organized, have demonstrated the great potential for empowerment that exists among women who are aware and committed to the promotion of well-being (i.e., *shalom*). Women in a village in India have been empowered to act on behalf of their environment by organizing the

Chipko (hug-the-tree) movement. In 1974, in Reni Village of the Garhwaal Himalaya, a group of women led by Gaura Devi hugged the trees, and thus challenged the hired sawyers, who were about to cut down the trees for a sports-goods company, to saw them alive first.[8]

In the Philippines, we have a similar story of women empowered to struggle for the well-being of their people. During the early years of martial law, the government entered into an agreement with the World Bank for a loan to build four dams in Northern Luzon that would provide irrigation for Central Luzon ricelands. This Chico River Dam project was rejected by the Bontoc and Kalinga peoples who regarded the area as their ancestral lands. One incident in the decade-long struggle (1973-1986) that finally resulted in President Aquino's indefinite postponement of the project, is of interest here. The women of the Bontoc and Kalinga tribes were the ones who approached the site where the engineers had set up their equipment and dispersed the men throwing their equipment over the side of the hill.

In both cases cited above, the women are engaged in the preservation of human well-being over technological progress. These women, therefore, become a source of empowerment for other women inspiring them to find creative ways of addressing other forms of peacelessness which threaten the well-being of human communities and their environment. It is this same concern for the well-being of the community, from within existing cultural mores, that we find displayed by biblical women. In order to be able to effectively reread the stories of these biblical women, however, we need to have some sense of the milieu within which these women functioned. To that end, we turn to a brief description of the world of biblical woman.

A Patriarchal World

The world of biblical women was a world in which power-over-others was exercised in the form of patriarchy. Patriarchy is defined as

> *a legal, social and economic system of society that validates and enforces the domination of male heads of families over the dependent persons in the household. In classical patriarchal systems, such as are found in Hebrew law, this included wives, dependent children and slaves.*[9]

As Sandra Schneiders points out, authority and power in the patriarchal system were "strictly coterminous and belonged totally and exclusively to the head of the household unless he delegated it to another".[10] In the patriarchal system, power, authority, property and maleness are vitally connected. While their opposites, powerlessness, exclusion from authority, dependence and femaleness are likewise closely linked.

> Patriarchy is the basic principle underlying not only the subordination of women to men, but of one race to another, of colonies to master nations, of children to adults, of nations to divine right monarchy, of believers to clergy. In other words, patriarchy is the nerve of racism, ageism, classism, colonialism, and clericalism as well as of sexism.[11]

Patriarchy, however, is not "natural" or inevitable, as anthropological scholarship has shown.

> It appears that patriarchal social systems arose with the first developments of large private landholding, the movement from gardening to animal-plowed agriculture, urbanization and class societies (including slavery) in approximately the beginning of the second millenium B.C. Before that (and alongside these patriarchal cultures) for at least a hundred thousand years, the predominant human patterns of hunting-gathering and hunting-gardening societies allowed for a more balanced community structure, and balanced productive spheres and powers of adult men and women.[12]

It is probably correct to say that biblical women did not challenge the patriarchal system as a system. But Danna Fewell gives several examples of biblical passages which invite us "to see not only the patriachal hierarchy but (also) how the hierarchy breaks down".[13]

There is, for example, the story in the first chapter of the Book of Esther which plainly demonstrates the fragility of male sovereignty and power. King Ahasuerus, after drinking about with cronies and friends, commands that Queen Vashti appear before the drunken rabble in her royal regalia in order to impress the crowd with her beauty. But the queen refuses. This unexpected challenge to his royal authority sends Kind Ahasuerus into a royal rage and he summons his wise men (who know the times) asking how Queen Vashti is to be treated according to the law 'because she has not performed the command of Kind Ahasuerus' (2:15). One of the wise men (who knew the times) replied:

> *Not only to the king has Queen Vashti done wrong, but also to all the princes and all the peoples who are in all the provinces of King Ahasuerus. For this deed of the queen will be made known to all women, causing them to look with contempt upon their husbands, since they will say, 'King Ahasuerus commanded Queen Vashti to be brought before him and she did not come.' This very day the ladies of Persia and Medea who have heard of the queen's behavior will be telling it to all the king's princes, and there will be contempt and wrath in plenty (2:166-18, RSV).*

Fewell comments, "the action (or perhaps I should say non-action) of one woman threatens to collapse the entire structure of patriarchy in the entire Persian empire."14

This passage from the Book of Esther shows male power and sovereignty to be dependent upon female acquiescence. Power is not an attribute, it is a relationship requiring a power-sender and a power-receiver. Queen Vashti's refusal to submit, to be a power-reciever, was rightly perceived as a threat to the power relationship of patriarchal dominance.

Fewell points to other biblical passages which show male sovereignty to be "incomplete, inadequate, and undesirable:"

> *Stories like those found in Genesis 27, in which Rebekah secures for Jacob the firstborn's blessing, and Genesis 38, in which Tamar takes her destiny into her own hands in spite of Judah's opposition to her, show the patriarch's perspective to be inaccurate and self-serving. The patriarch's control is a delusion. Stories like that of the rape of Dinah in Genesis 34 and the rape of Tamar in 2 Samuel 13 show that patriarchy cannot be depended upon for justice. Neither father Jacob nor father David lifts voice or finger to make restitution for his daughters, and the passive negligence of both fathers silently invites the violence that follows but that could have been avoided. Stories like the rape and dismemberment of the Levite's concubine in Judges 19 and the sacrifice of Jephthah's daughter in Judges 11 show the darkest side of patriarchy yet—the torture and murder of the most vulnerable and innocent for the sake of male honor and pompous religiosity.15*

Our reflection has shown the relational and dependent character of power as power-over-others. The biblical passages cited show that not all women of the biblical patriarchal period submitted without question to the existing arrangement.[16] It is passages such as these, rare in an androcentric or male-centered collection of religious traditions, that have the potential to empower women of faith to continue and even expand the struggle against vertical structures of interaction. It is these vertical structures, be they of sexism, racism, ageism, clericalism, militarism, imperialism or environmental degradation, that constitute the condition of peacelessness which characterizes our contemporary society. To struggle against them is a first state in building peaceful structures.

Empowerment of Women for Peace

The contemporary world is one in which the capacity for destruction has reached incredible proportions.[17] That which threatened *shalom* in biblical Israel was verbalized in the prophetic warnings of death by the triple threat of plague, famine and the sword of war. Translated into contemporary terminology, it could be said that the biggest challenge and threat facing the world today is the triple threat of ecocide, ethnocide and militarization.[18] The contemporary world is a world of paradoxes—it is a world of

> *overproduction and scarcity, of information explosion and increasing ignorance, of proliferation of commodities and shrinkage in nature's diversity, of affluence and poverty, of liberalization and human rights violation, of states that are at once too strong and too vulnerable. Ecological damage and cultural destruction are central to contemporary change.*
>
> *In cases of extreme tension, these paradoxical situations threaten the very foundations of peoples' lives as well as the planet itself. Ecocide and ethnocide are no longer imaginary scenarios created by doomsday prophets. They are happening; they are real. Together with militarization, they constitute the biggest challenge and threat faced by the world today.[19]*

In short, the dimensions of peacelessness characteristic of contemporary societies far exceed those of any previous societies.[20] One can only conclude that the dominant model of development, which had led to the replacement of a humane and good life as the organizing principles, has failed. An alternative vision which places human concerns at the center is urgently needed. As a major component of those segments of human society that have been rendered dispensable by the developmentalist state, women constitute an important resource for a recovery of the humane, the good and the just (i.e., for *shalom*) in society.

Since patriarchy has been the central core of the conceptual framework that has determined virtually all human interrelations and interactions for the last 5,000 to 6,000 years, we women have little or no practice in building peaceful structures. The task of building structures of peace thus requires a profound conceptual revolution, a *metanoia* (literally, a change of mindset). Perhaps because we are women we are particularly suited to this task, since we share with women everywhere and throughout history the reality of having been relegated to a secondary position in social life.

Awareness has been growing among women around the globe, and this includes women in various Asian societies, that the system that relegates women to a position of subordination is intimately interrelated with *all* other systems of dominance and subordination that deny people access to full participation in economic, political, cultural and religious life on the basis of ethnic derivation, race, gender, class or age. All of these dominance – subordination systems are maintained through violence and coercive force and are, therefore, manifestations of peacelessness.

Empowerment of women for peace, therefore, involves the awareness of existing dominance-subordination systems, the capacity to create a vision of an alternative to the prevailing social model, and the commitment to struggle toward bringing that alternative into being. As women of faith, we look to our biblical heritage as one source of empowerment in our effort to build peaceful structures in a world of inequitable interactions which constitute structural violence.

Within the limitations of the patriarchal framework, however, we have seen individual women offering individual challenges to the system. In the Book of Ruth, we also see women empowering one another toward a communal search for well-being, but within the framework of the existing patriarchal system. As the narrative begins, death abounds. After having left her homeland in a time of famine, Naomi finds herself bereft of husband and sons in a foreign land (1:5).

Upon hearing "that the Lord had visited his people and given them food" (1:6), Naomi set out to return to Bethlehem while advising for daughters-in-law to remain and marry in their own land. But Ruth refused to be separated from her mother-in-law and both women returned to Bethlehem where Naomi told the townswomen who met them at the gate: "I went away full, and the Lord has brought me back empty" (1:21).

Naomi is indeed empty, bereft of sons and husband, she lacks the male protection that provided security for women in patriarchal society. Lacking a male heir, she is destined for impoverishment—for a life of bitterness. "Why call me Naomi," she cries, "when the Lord has afflicted me and the almighty has brought calamity upon me" (1:21).

But soon the young Ruth is off in search of the gleanings which the law mandates should be left for 'the sojourner, the fatherless and the widow' (Deut 24:19-22). Coming, by accident, to the field of Boaz, a kinsman of Naomi's dead husband, Ruth sets in motion a process that will ultimately lead to the reversal of fortune for herself and her mother-in-law. As the narrative develops, the two women (unequal in age but sharing a common desire for personal well-being) mutually empower one another toward bringing about well-being for themselves.

As the story ends, Ruth has persuaded Boaz to perform his patriarchal responsibility by marrying her and providing a son for his kinsman, her dead husband. "So Boaz took Ruth and she became his wife; and he went in to her, and the Lord gave her conception, and she bore a son (4:13). Thus Naomi, who had called herself bitter (Mara), once again knew fullness and well-being in the land of her birth (4:14-17). The women of the town, the same who had greeted the two women upon their return to Bethlehem (1:19), acknowledge that this young Moabite woman has indeed been an occasion of blessing for Naomi: "Blessed be the Lord, who has not left you this day without next of kin' (4:14a). But more significantly, perhaps, the village women assert to Naomi that her dauther-in-law, who loves her, is more to her 'than seven sons' (vs 14b).

Separated, the two women are vulnerable to poverty and afflication, the lot of widows in patriarchal societies. Together they struggled, albeit within the existing patriarchal structure, to obtain personal well-being. In the process they brought well-being to the entire village and, ultimately, to the whole of Israel, as the son born to Ruth was destined to be the ancestor of David. David, that shepherd-boy turned bandit chief in the hills of Judah, would eventually defeat and sub-de the Philistines (2 Samuel 8:1), thus bringing temporary respite to the peoples in the villages harassed by Philistine troops (cf. I Sam 23:1).

The story of Ruth and Naomi is, among other things, a story of bonding and solidarity between two women who, had they gone their separate ways, most probably would not have found well-being for themselves, nor brought blessing upon their contemporaries (let alone on generations yet to come). As such the story has the capacity to suggest that an essential element in the empowerment of women for peace, or in other words, for social, economic, political, cultural and environmental well-being, is the bonding and solidarity of women across age, race, class and religion. The story also suggests the need to join with men in a concerted effort to see that the task of building structures of peace demands the building down of *all* vertical dominance-subordination structures.

We have seen that biblical *shalom* is a comprehensive concept not adequately rendered by the English "peace." While the world of the final decade of the 20th century is a much more complex world than that reflected in the biblical traditions, we must strive for the same wholistic concept of peace as *shalom*. As women of faith we have the responsibility to empower one another to constantly struggle to move the leadership of our respective nation-states beyond the short-sighted approach to peace that addresses complex socio-economic, political and cultural conflicts with military solutions. The increasingly lethal character of modern weapon systems demand from us the creativity of our sisters in the biblical tradition like Queen Vashti (who was not even an Israelite woman), Rebekah, Tamar and Ruth, and of our contemporary sisters from various tribal peoples who struggle to maintain their environment and culture against many odds. Through the stories of these women, and our solidarity in the struggle, may be empowered to continue, to struggle to bring about, what Johan Galtung terms, "a peacefare world of peacefare societies."21 &

ENDNOTES

[1]Riceour, Paul, "Creativity in Language," *Philosophy Today*. (1973). p. 111.

[2]See Exod 23:6, 21:2-11, 22:21-23, 22:27, Deut 15:1-11; etc.

[3]cf. Micah Chaps 1-3; Isa 5:1-7; 5:8-24 and 10:1-4 for example.

[4]Galtung, Johan. "Peace Theory: An Introduction," *World Encyclopedia of Peace*. Eds. Linus Pauline, Ervin Laszlo and John Youl Yoo. (New York: Perganon Press, 1986), p. 252.
See also a summary of definitions of peace in R.C. Musto. *The Catholic Peace Tradition*. (Maryknoll: Orbis, 1986), pp. 7-14.

[5]Galtung, Johan. *The True Worlds: A Transnational Approach*. (New York: Free Press, 1980), p. 62.

[6]*Ibid.*, p. 63.

[7]*Ibid.* See also Gene Sharp, *The Politics of Nonviolent Action*. (Boston: Porter Sargent Publishers, 1937), pp. 3-62.

[8]Shiva, 1988.

[9]Reuther, Rosemary R. "Church and Family in the Medieval and Reformation Periods." *New Blackfriars*, pp. 77-85. This article is the second in a series of five articles appearing January through May.
See also Schneiders, Sandra. *Women and the Word*. (Paulist Press: 1986), p. 11-14.

[10]Schneiders, p. 12.

[11]*Ibid.*, p. 13.

[12]Reuther, 1984, p. 78.
See also the comment of Betty Reardon that "authoritarian patriarchy, which seems to have emerged with the major elements of 'civilization'--- human settlements, organized agriculture, the state, and male domination--- invented and maintained war to hold in place the social order it spawned" (p. 12).

[13]Fewell, Danna Nolan. "Feminist Reading of the Hebrew Bible: Affirm-ation, Resistance and Transformation." JSOT 39:77-87, p. 82.

[14]Ibid, p. 83.

[15]Ibid, p. 84.

[16]On the other hand, not all women are (or are) conscious of how the patriarchal dominance system has affected their own interactions. The exer-cise of power-over-others can not simply be reduced to a gender problem. As

Fewell notes "the text calls us to mourn not only the victims, but the limited vision of those who victimize. And despite its patriarchal leanings, the Bible does not consistently assign gender to either of these roles" (p. 86).

[17]Johan Galtung makes reference to a 1974 statement of US senator Stuart Symington to the UN General Assembly that "the US nuclear stockpile is equal to 615,385 atomic bombs of the type dropped on Hiroshima in 1945. It is also claimed" Galtung continues, "that the United States has 7,000 nuclear bombs deployed in Europe and 3,000 in Asia, making a total of 10,000, to which one could add the estimate for the Soviet Union (2600), for China (200), for Britain (192), and France (86)--making a total of about 13,000 bombs. If the non-US bombs are of the same average strength, it should make a total of 800.000 Hiroshima bombs, and the one Hiroshima bomb we know killed 200,000 people. Given the same 'efficiency', the nuclear stockpile should be sufficient to kill 160 billion people, or forty times the world population" (Galtung: 1980, 239, n. 27).

[18]For more on militarization and militarism see the introductory section of "Militarization in the United States and the Soviet Union," *Alternatives* 10 (1984), pp. 93-113, and *idem.*, "Militarism and Militarization." Pp. 594-598 of *World Encyclopedia of Peace*. Eds. Linus Pauline, Ervin Laszlo & John Youl Yoo. New York: Pergamon Press, 1986.

[19]Kothari, Rajni. "On Humane Governance." *Alternatives.* (1987), p. 277.

[20]See Figure 1.1 The relations between belligerence and "civilization" in Johan Galtung. *The True Worlds*, p. 6. Galtung concludes that "there is something in 'civilization' that seems to go hand in hand with war" (ibid.). See also G. Lenski and J. Lenski, *Human Societies: An Introduction to Macrosociology.* 4th edition, (New York: McGraw-Hill, 1982).

[21]Galtung, 1980, p. 94.

WHO IS MARY?

Sr. Hilda Buhay, OSB

The history of the church in the Philippines is permeated by the presence of Mary. The idea is often premised that for us Filipinos, devotion to Mary is the most striking characteristic that can be said of our Catholic piety. Deep in every Filipino heart and enshrined in every Filipino home is the image of Mary as the object of veneration. The countless shrines of Mary in our country and the throng of devotees who flock to them to pay homage and plead for favors testify to a nation's singular affection to her. This is a grace but at the same time a challenge and a pastoral responsibility. Can we situate the Christian Filipino's image of Mary in the urgent task of liberating women from male domination as well as being in solidarity with the Filipino people's struggle for national sovereignty.

The Filipino's Image of Mary

Who is Mary to the Filipino? Mary is *Ang Mahal na Birhen* (the beloved virgin). She is the model of womanhood whose purity and chastity are worthy of emulation. Being *Ina ng Dios* (Mother of God) and *Inang Maawain* (Merciful Mother), relationship with Mary is expressed in petitions for her intercessory powers as an abundant source of merit and assistance when in straits. She is singularly blessed by God. Her sanctity is said to be the result of such "feminine" docility that it invited the highest graces from God. During the Spanish colonial period, the ideal Filipino woman was the *Maria Clara* type whose winsome feminine qualities were commonly perceived as resembling those of Mary. Maria Clara may long be dead but our society still puts a premium on submission, blind obedience and passivity in Filipino women. Mary then, when imitated, becomes an extremely useful means of domesticating women and other oppressed people.

Mary--an impossible model in the context of injustice today?

Popular church prayers present Mary in a dazzling litany of praise—Virgin most Faithful, Mother most Powerful, Mother of Divine Grace, Mirror of Justice, Seat of Wisdom, Mystical Rose and so on. What aspects of Mary's character can we identify with, after religious traditions and piety have raised her "up there", far removed from the struggle of people "here below?" Given the socio-economic and moral decline occurring in our country today, what can vulnerable, broken and dehumanized human beings know of the wholeness of grace, purity, power and fidelity? Can we ever hope to mirror justice and to make this world a more human place to live in? Is Mary, after all, an impossible model of life for us in our contemporary conditions? Shall we have to remain the *Inang Maawain* we have put on the altar of glories to whom we go as the source of perpetual succor? Shall we stop short of extolling the *Mahal na Birhen* for her physical virginity and "using' her to legitimize our difference and non-involvement in the care of those who suffer degradation and injustice? We must question the average Filipino's image of Mary further. Does this image make sense in view of the irruption of men and people's power today? Does the symbol of Mary give meaning and offer inspiration in the work for conscientization and social justice today?

We have to re-read the Scriptures to reappropriate Mary's role in people's lives today, to re-capture more realistic signs of Mary and discover anew her historical place in a liberating Church. The biblical view of Mary as one of our race, so close to us in her refreshing humanity, so clearly identified with our world of conflicts in her understanding and solidarity.

Mary of Nazareth, a woman of faith

Who was Mary of Nazareth as depicted in the Scriptures? The Jewish woman Mary—of what stuff was she made of? Mary is the image of a young Jewish woman unadorned by the glorious title that popular religiosity has bestowed on her in the quality of her relationships. She has the same stuff of which we are made. She is our sister in faith.

Biblical scholars unanimously agree that Mary's witness to us in Scripture is a witness of faith. The simple announcement of God's coming in time (Lk. 1:26-28) is met by the single-minded trait of this woman who had lived in the stream of God's promise in the history of her humiliated people. Mary's response, "Be it done to me according to your word" is often interpreted as a passive, unquestioning acceptance of God's will. It will make matters worse when this kind of model is held up for the poor, for women particularly, because it reinforces their subordinate position in the family, society and in the church. Mary's receptivity does not imply powerlessness nor is it simply a passive trait. It is rather the creative submission of the fully liberated human being, who—not being subject to any other human being or human law—is free to serve God.

By the same token, Mary's *fiat* shows that receptivity includes an active element. Because Mary's *fiat* was truly responsible, it had the capacity to deepen and mature intensely. We can only glean the ascent of different situations in the unfolding of the Mystery of Christ in her life. Each of these crises was an acute experience of human limitations and struggle in the face of the inscrutible design of God. The birth of Jesus, the visit of the wisemen, the flight into Egypt and the loss of the twelve-year-old Jesus in the temple are accounts that suggest critical phases in Mary's personal life. The allusion of Scripture to her growth in discerning faith is simple and without dramatics "...and this mother kept all these things in her heart" (Lk 2:19). At the crucifixion scene, the Fourth Gospel narrates that Mary stood her ground at the foot of the cross (Jn 19:25-27). Truly valuable is this insight in the humaness of Mary's own struggle for us who need courage to face the twists of human life and the challenges posed by critical periods in the history of our people.

Another image of Mary—the woman for others—is presented by the evangelist John in the narrative of the Wedding of *Cana* (Jn 2). It is the figure of Mary expressing to her Son her genuine concern for the needs of the bridal couple at the feast. This natural involvement of Mary in a concrete problem that arose in that situation does not in the least catch us by surprise for it is the same active concern which we have met earlier in Luke when Mary visited her cousin Elizabeth. Openness and sensitivity to God became truly credible in Mary's case because she reached out to embrace her neighbors. Mary of Nazareth is projected here as a woman who has a keen eye for the needs of a particular situation and is quick to assess a problematic situation and share in the search for its solution.

From such accounts, we can deduce conclusions of Mary's attitude as a person which reveals her authentic human sensibilities. Her genuine human touch has been a powerful reflector of justice and integrity, qualities badly needed as a counter-culture in our society today. Thus, Mary of Nazareth is someone who can serve as a model even in our age, because of her experience with the God of her faith, her history as an ordinary person. Such a model is needed today if we are to concern ourselves with work for justice for women who are kept in subservience, for slum dwellers who are evicted, for political detainees who are tortured, farmers, workers and other oppressed members of our society.

Mary of the Magnificat, a woman of commitment

How does the figure of Mary serve as the reference point in the light of our evangelical task of the evangelization of our people? We can refer to her identity as a Jewish girl steeped in the traditions of Israel and in the concerns of the historical struggles of her people as chosen people of Yahweh. We who are readers of the Old Testament cannot miss the importance of Jewish national history as a constitutive element in the national consciousness of every God-fearing member of the race of Israel.

That Mary is a conscientized Jewish girl, conscious of her nation's history and national faith is documented for us in the Lucan account of Mary's Magnificat (Lk 1:46-55):

> My soul doth magnify the Lord (sic)
> and my spirit rejoices in God my Savior
> for he (sic) has regarded the lowliness of his (sic) handmaid
> for behold all generations shall call me blessed
> for he (sic) who is mighty has done great things for me
> and holy is his (sic) name
> His (sic) mercy is from generation to generation
> unto them who fear him (sic)
> He (sic) hath put down the mighty from their throne
> and exalted the lowly
> He (sic) filled the hungry with good things
> and sent the rich away empty
> He (sic) hath received his (sic) servant Israel
> being mindful of his (sic) mercy
> As he (sic) promised to our Father,
> to Abraham and to his children forever. (Lk. 1:46-55)

One can choose to hear this song as Mary's individual hymn of praise. However, Mary must have sung her Magnificat in broad national and historical perspectives. Her song must have been a song bursting out of the heartstrings of an oppressed people, the *anawim*. It was a song of exaltation in the final liberation of Yahweh, of His people. In this, Mary shows she is not alien to the suffering of her nation. She is not stranger to the patriotic sentiments of the chosen people of God.

The Magnificat is not just a pious song. Today one hears such sentiments only from the revolutionary. It can therefore be one of the inspirations for Christian women in their struggle for a fuller humanity. Mary was concerned about the transfer of power and problems of inequality. Being a woman with a sense of history who bravely related her experience with the history of her people and assumed the historical task, we could say that the exemplary potential of Mariology is open to this consideration of her commitment to the social destiny of her people.

Conclusion

Who is Mary?

Biblical reflections of the images of Mary point to her as the Jewish woman of witness, unflinching faith and sterling humanity. She is the conscientized and committed Jewish woman who sang of solidarity in struggle with the poor and the oppressed in the Magnificat. Mary is not an impossible model in the Philippine context of injustice today. Christian Filipinos must be liberated from the traditional stereo-typed images of Mary drawn from popular Marian piety. People who seek deep commitment in service to the kingdom can draw much inspiration from the Mary of the Scriptures. ✧

THE RELIGIOUS WOMAN TODAY AND INTEGRAL EVANGELIZATION

Sr. Mary John Mananzan, OSB

Introduction

In most third world countries today, an understanding of salvation and evangelization is effecting radical changes in Christian praxis and is therefore transforming the self-understanding, life style and missionary orientation, approach and methods of religious communities.

Such an understanding of salvation in a land where injustice and oppression abide makes a challenge out of a Christian's life. To be a religious woman in such a situation is doubly so. It calls for radically re-thinking the meaning of being a Christian and of the imperatives of religious commitment. It precipitates a spiritual crisis and demands a consequent revision of one's way of life.

Salvation and Integral Evangelization

The principal message of Christianity is the good news of salvation. For a long time in the history of the Church the idea that salvation meant almost exclusively the salvation of the soul—its salvation from death, sin and hell—has prevailed. Missionary reports would speak primarily of "so many thousands of souls saved." The main missionary tasks were preaching the word of God and dispensing the sacraments: everything else that the missionary did for the people's "material welfare" was considered "pre-evangelization."

The current understanding of salvation, on the other hand, sees salvation as the liberation of the whole human being, not only from sin, death and hell but from everything that dehumanizes him including oppression, exploitation, injustice, poverty. This is to be achieved by a process called integral evangelization, preaching the Gospel in the context of the total environment—economic, political, social—considering the historical factors that affect human destiny. This understanding of evangelization and salvation presupposes a theology that is incarnated in the specific historical and local context of a people—a theology that is aware of the structural concatenations of the society in which it moves, and one that reflects upon the significant human events that happen among the people in the light of the Gospel.

Biblical Perspective

In reality, this total view of salvation is not really new. Fr. Carlos Abesamis, SJ, one of the few original Filipino theologians, has developed a theology of total salvation which traces salvation through the different periods of the Old Testament to the early Church.[1]

In his diachronic study of the understanding of salvation, Abesamis shows that in the Israelitic Period, salvation was concrete. It primarily meant the Exodus experience, the liberation from the bondage of Egypt, the covenant, the promised land—what they called the *Mirabilia Dei*, Yahweh's deeds of salvation. And such salvation, Abesamis writes, "was not the salvation of the soul from sin but the bestowing of the blessings that affect the totality of life of an Israelite and of the Israelitic nation."

The prophetic shared this basic insight regarding salvation being concrete and total. In this period, Deutero-Isaiah announced the liberation for the exiled Jews in Babylon, Jeremiah spoke of the coming home of the scattered sons of Israel. Ezechiel announced that Yahweh will give his people a new heart and a new spirit. The new element was the foretelling of God's final definitive saving action.

The Jewish apocalyptic writers would believe in the same basic understanding but would further clarify it by giving it a cosmic dimension—a "new heaven and a new earth where there will be no more mourning nor tears nor pain nor death."

Christ himself did not "spiritualize" salvation. When John sent his disciples to him and asked if he were the promised Messiah, he answered them: "Go and tell John what you hear and see: the blind receive their sight and the lame walk, lepers are cleansed, the deaf hear and the dead are raised up and the poor have the good news preached to them." (Mt. 11: 4-5)

And there was the dramatic incident at the synagogue when after being handed the scroll of the prophet Isaiah, he read the part:

The spirit of the Lord has been given to me,
for he has anointed me.
He has sent me to bring the good news to the poor,
to proclaim liberty to captives
and to the blind new sight,
to set the downtrodden free,
to proclaim the Lord's year of favour.

Then he announced: "This text is being fulfilled today even as you listen" (Luke 4:18-21). In Christ, salvation has begun yet it remains uncompleted. Total salvation in him has the dimension of the "already now" and the "not yet" and it is precisely because of this that the Church has a mission to work for the fulfillment of their total salvation.

But what happened between then and now? How did the spiritualized view of salvation assume dominance?

Philosophico - Historical Perspective

Christianity has an asset which also constitutes its vulnerability—namely its historicity. Christ was incarnated at a certain time, among a people in a particular place. His Church likewise grew in time, among peoples, within cultures. In its early years of growth, Christianity found itself flourishing in the Hellenistic culture of the Graeco-Roman world. It was understandable that the early Fathers of the Church steeped in this culture explained and spread the teachings of Christianity in the conceptual framework in which they found themselves. They used the categories of Greek philosophy, especially that of Plato, in their explanation and exposition of Christianity. It is not strange therefore that Platonic dualism would now influence Christian thought. Platonic dualism took three forms: Metaphysical—the dualism of two worlds, the real world of ideas and the phenomenal world of the senses. Epistemological—the dualism of two forms of knowledge, the real innate knowledge of the world of ideas, and opinion or sense of knowledge; and Psychological—the dualism of body and soul.

It should be noted that this dualistic view of the human being persisted throughout the Middle Ages and received a new impetus in the dualism of Descartes in the 16th Century. With him, there was a complete dichotomy of human consciousness and the world, between subject and object, between thought and reality. Post-Cartesian philosophy branched out from one assumption of the body-soul dichotomy into two extreme positions namely, idealism and materialism absolutizing either spirit (in the case of idealism) or matter (in the case of materialism).

Christianity in its theology and spirituality would for a long time be influenced by idealism. Hence, the almost exclusive concern for the soul, the denigration of the body, the suspicious outlook on the world (*fuga mundi*).

Twentieth century philosophy is basically a reaction to Platonic dualism. It stressed the existential unity of body and soul; it stressed that the human being is necessarily a worldly human being and the world is essentially a human world. In contrast to the essentialism of the doctrine of truth existing in a world of ideas, contemporary-philosophy pointed to the historicity of human truth. This further intensified the growing movement of secularity which demanded that the world be taken seriously.

There was a popular saying during the reign of Louis XIV that when "France sneezes Europe catches cold." Here one can adopt the saying and claim that "when philosophy sneezes, theology catches cold." The changes in viewing the human being and the world cannot but influence theological thought.

Ecclesial Perspective

The changes in the Church's thinking was first felt in the documents of Vatican II especially in the document, *Gaudium et Spes*. Here there is a positive view of the world, a serious discussion of people's economic, political, and social needs and an endorsement of involvement in one's world. Since then, Church documents like *Pacem in Terris*, *Populorum Progressio*, Justice in the World, *Evangelii Nuntiandi* have explained in greater detail one's responsibilities in relation to other people and the world. In its reading of the signs of the times, the Church, represented by the Synod of

Bishops in Rome in 1971, perceived "serious injustices which are building around the world of men a network of domination, oppression and abuses which stifle freedom and which keep the greater part of humanity from sharing in the building up and enjoyment of a more just and more fraternal world" (Justice in the World, Introduction). However, the document also showed signs of a "new awareness which shakes them out of any fatalistic resignation and which spurns them on to liberate themselves... It is in this context that the bishops proclaim: "Action in behalf of justice and participation in the transformation of the world fully appears to us as a constitutive dimension of the preaching of the Gospel".

This is not synonymous to saying that justice is the supreme Christian virtue. Love remains the apex of the Christian life. But what remains clear is that it is impossible to have true love without justice. Justice is the foundation of love. This concept is emphasized today because the network of domination, exploitation, oppression and other forms of injustice have so poisoned the atmosphere that there is no room for Christian love to thrive. Christian love necessarily had to take the form of creating the climate for itself by bringing about justice in human relationships and in social structures.

Religious Commitment Today

It is in this light that the commitment of the religious woman today will be discussed. Anyone who enters the religious life whether through teaching, nursing, doing social work, etc. commits herself primarily to the preaching of the Gospel in her words and deeds, in her life. If action in behalf of justice is a constitutive dimension of preaching the Gospel today, any religious woman who is unconcerned with justice cannot be said to be living her commitment.

What precisely consists this concern for justice? If we study the dynamics of injustice we shall see that the victims of injustice are the materially poor—those who have little or no control of economic resources and therefore, have little or no control of the decision-making processes that affect their lives. Concern for justice therefore means first and foremost an option for the materially poor. But it is not enough to have a sympathetic, affective concern for the poor, one must be effectively concerned. And today when we are more knowledgeable about economic and political structures we can no onger limit our concern for the poor in dole - outs, not even in developmental projects, but we have to come to grips with structural obstacles. The effectivity of one's concern is measured by one's willingness to confront these obstacles and bring about structural changes.

Concern for justice further entails the readiness to defend human rights and to engage in effective action against the gross violation of these rights.

At this point I have to cite my own experience as a religious woman in the Philippines to illustrate the concrete consequences of this new theologizing.

The Societal Context of My Commitment

Throughout the years, Philippine society has been plagued with two basic economic problems; namely, the unequal distribution of resources—2% of its population controls 75% of its land and capital—and foreign control of its economy through foreign transnational corporations and through its foreign debt which now amounts to 29 billion dollars. The elite class controls not only the economic system but the political and ideological apparatus of society as well. The people's consciousness reflects the elite's values and interests expressed in mass media, in an uncritical educational system and the conservative teachings and practices of the Churches.

The famous EDSA Event caused the downfall of a 20-year dictatorship but it did not end the misery of the people. It changed the head of the nation but not the ruling class, nor the repressive political machinery with its military components. The new administration adapted the same orientation in its economic development model. In other words, no social revolution took place. Consequently the core problems of the people remain. These in turn perpetuate massive poverty with 75% of the people living below the poverty line and suffering from malnutrition, brain damage, unemployment and underemployment, brain and muscle drain. These problems also give way to chronic insurgency and intensifying militarization which has cost many Filipino lives.

Baptism of Fire

In 1975, this was the same situation of crisis, oppression

and injustice that made me respond to a telephone brigade asking nuns, seminarians and priests to come to the rescue of 600 striking workers from La Tondeña, a wine factory. It was the first attempted strike after the strike ban was issued following the declaration of Martial Law in September, 1972.

I had just come from a 6-year study leave in Germany and Rome and I was teaching Contemporary Philosophy in the Jesuit University. I joined a group called "Interfaith Theological Circle" that aimed at evolving a "Filipino Theology" in the air-conditioned library of the University. Needless to say, we were criticized as engaging in "intellectual gymnastics" despite the extremely erudite papers we produced on the subject. After a period of defensiveness, we realized that it was indeed futile to evolve such a theology without getting involved in the struggle of the people. This was what made me respond to the invitation of the La Tondena workers. There I had my first encounter with military brutality and I experienced helplessness, having to face the reality of force and institutional violence. That was where we established the "Friends of the Workers."

The La Tondeña strike inspired other strikes, more than 100 in a period of three months, and we went from one factory to the other, gaining valuable learning experiences from the people, getting an insight into the root causes of their problems. We were immersed in the problems of slum dwellers, too, for the workers lived in slums. We joined human barricades to stop demolitions. We formed composite groups that spearheaded rallies and marches. We were recruited into negotiating teams to face the military in mass actions. And inevitably we got involved in the fate of political detainees who were arrested in marches, rallies and pickets, and who were snatched from their houses in midnight raids.

The Anguish of Awareness

This initiation into the struggles of the people shook the framework of my Christian and religious existence. I quote at length an article I wrote describing this experience:

"Social awareness can mean real anguish. Exposures to the miseries of our people even on a minor scale and a serious reflection on these experiences can confront us with facts that would question our former values. And yet it takes time to adopt and synthesize the new set of values that one begins to perceive. One is back to

zero during this period. One is barren. One stops giving talks or writing articles, because one feels empty, one needs to be re-educated. This awareness gives one a sense of urgency that may seem fanatic to those who either do not see or who confine social consciousness to community assemblies. Here is where one can make a mistake in strategy and become over-zealous and turn off people. But there is indeed a constriction of the heart which one feels when one talks with people who see no further than the four protective walls of their houses or convents. Here is where awareness can cause real loneliness. All of a sudden one is on a different plane when talking with one's family, one's closest friends and colleagues. Not to be able to share values can be a painful form of isolation. The slow, painstaking trial and error attempts to share these new values and new imperatives without turning people off can bring one to a point of helplessness and frustration, further aggravated by one's clearer and closer perception of the problem's magnitude and the uncertain risks and corresponding magnitude of the proposed solutions. Time and time again, to confront in others one's own prejudice, blind spots, and doubts, is to relive one's own metanoia without the sense of relief at the thought that the decision and choice lies within one's power. But perhaps the greatest anguish is the yawning gap between one's insight and one's generosity. Insight brings with it imperatives to action that may mean crucial decisions and to perceive and yet not to have the courage or moral energy to act is a real agony. To conscientize is truly a serious business, because the price of awareness is anguish.[2]

To take stock of things and to understand what was happening to themselves, 30 priests and sisters initiated an alternative retreat which they called *Hakbang* (step forward). *Hakbang* was a 5-day retreat which paved the way for sharing in-depth experiences of how they got involved, their anxieties, doubts, apprehensions, fears, hopes. It also enabled the analysis of both the society and the Church and the formulation of visions for a transformed society and a renewed church. Each day was climaxed by a creative liturgy that recapitulated the sharing sessions. This alternative retreat was repeated for other groups. The result was a leveling of consciousness, a greater clarity of vision, a renewed courage borne out of common experiences, of personal liberation, and a greater motivation to go forward.

Commitment to Women's Concerns

The feminist movement is new in the Philippines. Although already concerned with prostitution in the Philippines. I did not get involved in the feminist movement until 1978 when I was invited to a World Council of Churches Conference on Human Rights and Women in Venice. When I returned to the Philippines I co-founded the *Filipina*, the first organization of women with a conscious and expressedly feminist orientation. With other women I established the Center for Women's Resources (CWR). In 1984, CWR took the initiative to call a conference of all women's organizations that mushroomed at that time. In this conference, the federation of women's organizations, GABRIELA, was born. It is now the most extensive federation of women in the Philippines counting 100 member organizations and about 40,000 individual members. In 1986, I was elected its National Chairperson and was re-elected for a period of 2 years in 1987.

GABRIELA has clearly defined the orientation of the women's movement in a third world country like the Philippines. It sees women's liberation within the context of the economic, political and cultural transformation of society. This is the necessary though not sufficient condition of women's liberation. There is no total human liberation without the liberation of women in society. And this is not an automatic consequence of either economic development or political revolution. In other words, the women's movement is an essential aspect of the process of societal liberation.

GABRIELA makes use of seven main strategies to achieve its goals. The most important is organization, because oppressed groups are empowered only by organization. GABRIELA is organized according to sectors, regions and areas of interests. Mobilization of GABRIELA members along national issues such as foreign bases, foreign debts, consumer issues, etc, is very important. GABRIELA also initiates campaigns on specific women's concerns such as prostitution, mail-order brides and domestic violence. The third strategy is education, both formal and informal, institutional and non-institutional. It is of utmost importance to awaken the awareness of women to their situation because the great majority of women have internalized their oppression. The fifth strategy, feminist scholarship, differs from education by its emphasis on the development of the women's perspective in the different academic disciplines, like Psychology,

Theology, History, etc. The legal strategy has achieved a major victory when the women's campaign on women's rights resulted in the inclusion of the equal rights provision in the newly ratified Philippine Constitution. For women who are victims of violence, crisis centers are being established for legal, medical, and psychological aid. The urban poor women in slum areas have been assisted by livelihood projects, day care centers and primary health care clinics. These constitute the welfare strategy. Finally, the women believe in an international solidarity strategy because the women's cause is a universal cause. Every year the international desk of **GABRIELA** organizes a **WISAP (Women International** Solidarity Affair in the Philippines) Conference attended by women from different parts of the world.

As a religious *woman*, my commitment to the oppressed which started with political militancy developed into a commitment for the struggle of women against gender oppression. Again, being a *religious* woman brought my attention to the religious roots of women oppression. Together with Asian women coming from different religious and cultural backgrounds, we came to the insight that all religions have oppressive as well as liberating elements which could serve for or against women. So far, more of the oppressive factors have been used to rationalize and justify the continued subordination of women. The agenda for renewal consists of making the liberating forces of religion operative in the lives of women.

Religious Spirituality Emerging from Commitment

Involvement in the struggles of people brings one to a spiritual crisis. I have described the anguish that comes with initial awareness and the costly consequences of commitment. One goes into the soul's dark night (*noche oscura*) and when one emerges, one experiences a shakeup in one's spirituality which may result either in "giving up one's faith" (some of my friends have made this option) or undergoing a real *metanoia*.

The first effect of this conversion is the rethinking of one's concept of the religious life. I wrote:

> But even while turning her attention to these actions
> for justice, the religious has likewise to rethink her
> religious life, her vows, her spirituality and lifestyle

according to the insight that justice is a constituent dimension of her being a Christian and religious.

The vow of poverty takes on more flesh and blood than the usual economizing or asking of permission. Poverty today must be truly experienced in the surrender of vested interests, in genuine simple living, and if possible, in "pitching one's tent" among the poor. At the very least it would demand an unreserved sharing of one's resources with the poor and the oppressed.

Obedience can take on a new dimension in letting one's role be defined by the needs of the people. The vox populi, vox Dei *adage takes on a new reality. One begins to listen to people with the ear of one's heart instead of dictating to them or taking the leading role. Just as there is personal and communal poverty, there is, likewise personal and communal obedience. Congregations and religious communities have to learn to obey the signs of the times. They learn to insert themselves meaningfully into the local Church where they find themselves.*[3]

The spirituality that emerges from the involvement with the struggles of the oppressed shows, in my experience, four trends... It is spirituality that is liberational, integral, feminist, and oriental.

During the *Hakbang* or alternative retreat of the religious activists mentioned in the beginning of the paper, each one shared his/her journey to commitment and the remarkable consensus was that each one experienced an inner liberation. Christ, the fully liberated person became the inspiration. The involvement with oppressed people contributes to self-knowledge and self-acceptance which become the basis of an inner liberation which manifests itself in a growing freedom from fear, from idols, and from bitterness and resentment. Freedom from fear does not consist in not feeling fear but in the ability to distinguish between groundless fear and substantiated fear and to act in spite of substantiated fear. One becomes less worried about what an "anonymous they" might be thinking or criticizing. Besides being free from this "negative idol" one also experiences a freedom from legalism and from sacralizing law or from being enslaved to positive idols that one had put on pedestals during one's life. While acknowledging the bitterness and resentment in one's negative experiences, one begins to transcend them and transform them into a creative and positive resolution of one's problems.

There is also a remarkable simplification of one's faith and one's practices. There is an integration of the vertical and horizontal dimensions of one's religious life. To elaborate:

> "It is understandable that one's spirituality will be influenced by this new thrust or else there will be a painful dichotomy." One's life of prayer will be "invaded" by the anguish of people. The psalms take on a relevance in confrontation with new Pharoahs and new Egypt or the need for a new Exodus and a new Promised Land. Liturgy will have to echo the crying aspirations of the oppressed as much as the joy of every step toward their liberation. The ascetism of the religious committed to justice need not be contrived. It will be imposed on her by the difficult situation that will inevitably arise: the demands of people that cannot be put on a rigidly controlled time table or calendar; in the expected persecution from the rich and powerful whose vested interests will be endangered; and in the misunderstandings of friends and loved ones who would be threatened by one's radicality. [4]

The feminist perspective to spirituality developed as women started to reflect on their experiences as women, both personal and social, as well as on their common struggle against their manifold oppression. This spirituality is nourished by their growing understanding of their self-image which has been obscured by the roles that have been assigned to them by a patriarchal society. This in turn influences their interpersonal relationships and touches the collective consciousness that is growing among them as they struggle against exploitation and discrimination. It is shaped by the victories which they have achieved in their struggle. Women's emerging spirituality is therefore not just a vertical relationship with God but it is an integral one. it is shaped not only by prayer but by relational experience and struggle—personal, interpersonal and societal.

The release of creative energy and the new insights in the women's struggle have likewise affected a new focus and new expressions of spirituality. It is creation-centered rather than sin- and redemption-centered. It is holistic rather than dualistic. It is risk rather than security. It is a spirituality that is joyful rather than austere, active rather than passive, expansive rather than limiting. It celebrates more than it fasts; it lets go more than it holds back. It is an Easter rather than a Good Friday spirituality. It is vibrant, liberating and colorful.

The holistic aspect that feminist influence has exerted on spirituality has likewise given rise to a newly observed phenomenon among activists in the Philippines, and that is the reclaiming of the contemplative heritage of Asia's great religions. Social activitists in the Philippines are taking up the practice of Zen which they undertake with the same zeal as they take up causes. Ruben Habito explaines that the term spirituality equates with the Greek *pneuma* (spirit) which in turn equates with the Hebrew *Ruah*, the Breath of God. Throughout the Old and New Testaments, the Breath of God plays a key role in all the events of salvation history from creation to the incarnation. Habito then shows the relationship between Zen practice and social militancy:

> *Paying attention to one's breathing in Zen... is seen not simply as a physical exercise that keeps one concentrated on one point, but as the very abandonment of one's total being to this Breath of God, here and now. It is letting one's whole self be possessed by the Spirit of God, to be vivified, guided, inspired, and fulfilled in it.*

> *And as one is "overshadowed" by the Spirit, one's whole being is offered for God's dynamic liberating action in history, to preach the good news to the poor. To proclaim release to the captives. To set at liberty those who are oppressed.*[5]

In another way of expressing this, Sr. Elaine MacInnes writes of the socially significant effect of Zen practice:

> *Our dissipated energies gradually become more unified and we start to gain some control over our super active mind. Tensions are released, nerves are relaxed, and physical health generally improves. Emotions are sensitized. We begin to experience a kind of inner balance and gradually dryness, rigidity, hangups, prejudice, egoism, melt and give way to compassion, serenity, egolessness and social concern.*[6]

The *koan* method presents the Zen student with "riddles" which the intellect will repel but which is grasped by the self-nature in an intuitive response. The student soon comes to see that everyday life is a koan which invites response. As Sr. Elaine further writes. When we see someone thirsty, we give a drink. When we are confronted with injustice, we cannot remain unmoved.[7]

This recourse to oriental mysticism for the social activists closes the full circle of action—contemplative action.

Conclusion

Being a religious woman today is more difficult, more demanding but definitely more challenging. When I hear a young woman answer the question "Why do you want to enter the convent?" with "Because I want to have peace and quiet," I just smile.

The religious life has come a long way from the *fuga mundi* principle of the early days of monasticism. Religious women who were particularly the objects of enclosure laws of Canon Law because they were not only *religious* but *women*, have emerged from these constraints and have become involved in the burning issues of society and in some cases have been on the forefront of militant causes.

Personally, I find being a religious woman in a third world country a dangerous but challenging and meaningful existence. If forces one to go back to the original meaning of the core of the Christian message. Impelled by a sense of urgency because of the living experience of people's sufferings and oppression, religious women are inspired to a consequent living out of this Christian imperative in the concrete struggles of their world. This in turn gives them an experiential insight into the meaning of the paradox of committed freedom. The religious woman committed to justice becomes truly convinced that to seek her life is to lose it and to lose her life is to gain it, not only for herself but for others—for those who will perhaps see the fulfillment of her vision of a better world, something she will probably not see in her own lifetime. ⊞

ENDNOTES

1Carlos Abesamis, "Total Salvation, Key to Understanding the Mission of the Church in Asia Today," an unpublished manuscript.

2Mary John Mananzan, Editorial in *Conversation*, Sept., 1975.

3Mary John Mananzan, "The Religion Today & Integral Evangelization" in *Lumen Vitae*, Vol. XXXI, 1976, pp. 321-322.

[4] Mary John Mananzan. "Woman & Religion" in *Religion & Society.* (Manila: Fides, Publication, 1988), p. 119.

[5] Ruben Habito. "Spirituality: Alluring to the Breath of God," in *Asia's Gift to a Total Christian Spirituality.* (Manila: Zen Center for Oriental Spirituality in the Philippine, 1988), p. 7.

[6] Sr. Elaine MacInnes. "What is Oriental Spirituality" in *Ibid.*, p. 5.

[7] Loc Cit.

A PRACTICE OF ECUMENISM AMONG CHURCH WOMEN

Sr. Mary John Mananzan, OSB

Introduction

Ever since the break-up of the Church into different confessions and sects, it has been the dream of many Christians to bring about unity in the Church. Missionaries especially feel the scandalized reactions of non-Christians when confronted with the differences, and even at times enmities, between people who all proclaim to be the followers of Christ.

The history of ecumenism shows that for a long time the ecumenical initiative has come from the Protestant Churches beginning from the various efforts and conferences (Stockholm 1925; Oxford 1937; Geneva 1920; Lausanne 1927; Oxford and Edinburg in 1937) that culminated in the foundation of the World Council of Churches in 1948 in Amsterdam.

The Roman Catholic Church, although it sent observers to the Third Assembly of the WCC in New Delhi, began serious efforts at ecumenism only at the impulse of Vatican II and with the establishment of the Secretariat for Christian Unity in 1960.[1]

From the efforts of the ecumenical movement arose an ecumenical theology within the last 25 years which is a self-reflection of the theological thinking confronting the reality of the disunity in the Church. It tackles the question of dialogue and cooperation between the different denominations.

In the Philippines which is a predominantly Catholic country, there has been for a long time no real effective effort at ecumenism. We can still recall the time when it was considered "mortal sin" for a Catholic to enter a Protestant church, much more so if one attended a Protestant worship service. There is no noteworthy record of theological discussions among the churches except for articles written on ecumenism which are theoretical and rather universal or at most Asian in application but not actually applicable to the Philippine situation. [2] What perhaps could be considered a noteworthy impulse toward ecumenism were the efforts documented in the November 22, 1970 issue of Sunday Times Magazine which adopted the theme of ecumenism on the occasion of Pople Paul VI's visit to the Philippines.

It is perhaps only in the last 5 years or so that ecumenism in the Philippines experienced a qualitative leap. It is the objective of this article to document a manifestation of that leap in connection with ecumenism among church women. Note that the title of the article says "a practice of ecumenism" because this article does not purport to document all the ecumenical efforts among church women in the Philippines, but just the phase in which the author has been involved.

The New Factor in Ecumenism

Before we go to an actual description of the ecumenical work among church women it is good to contextualize this in the broader framework of what the author considers as a qualitative leap in ecumenism in the country.

The impulse that brought about this impetus in the years surrounding the declaration of Martial Law in 1972 is economic and socio-political in nature. Already in the articles written in the Sunday Times issue on Ecumenism cited above, we read:

> ...ecumenism must be considered a liberative force for meaningful socio-economic national development and not merely a recognition of the brotherhood of all men of all creeds at all times... Ecumenism should help expose the spiritual and material exploitation of the masses of our people... [3]

And from Bishop Yap in the same issue:

> Protestants and Catholics can work together on points that they agree even though they disagree in some points... In social action programs for example, the two can work together.[4]

It is this external impulse propelled by the economic and socio-political conditions that indeed brought ecumenism in the Philippines to a new phase. Church people, being confronted by worsening conditions of society, diverted and focused their attention on a common crisis. Immediately the declaration of Martial Law in 1972 when all militant opposition groups had to lie low, church people found themselves at the forefront of the movement, faced with the unique opportunity of fulfilling their prophetic role. As such they were forced to seriously study the situation and church people of different confessions sat side by side struggled to produce a common reading of the situation. Some even arrived at common political options that further eliminated religious obstacles to ecumecial cooperation. They met each other in the same exposure areas and the same panel at symposia, linked arm-in-arm at demonstrations or pickets, conscientization seminars and community organizing projects, and worked together in the same committee for some special task. Even such a sensitive area as worship became a practical meeting point, because for some time it was only in common worship that they could give expression to their grievances. Such ecumenical services were branded by some as "making use of the liturgy" but was regarded by others as giving supreme expression to what liturgy is all about—public worship—worship of the people, reminiscent of the groanings of the people of Israel in their Exodus experience.

Another development in the late '70s and early '80' that would influence ecumenism among women was the advent of feminism in the Philippines. Before the '70s there was no explicit feminist orientation. However by the early '80s women's organizations while a definite feminist orientation mushroomed in the Philippines. A highpoint was the formation of a National Federation of these organizations—the GABRIELA. Included in this federation were ecumenical groups of church women.

Forms of Ecumenism among Church Women

It is in this new atmosphere of openness that ecumenism among church women also bloomed.

In a consultation of church women in Dasmariñas, Cavite which adapted as theme "Church Women: Speak, Lead, Share", an ecumenical association of women was born taking the name Philippine Association of Theologically Trained Women (PATH-TWO). Its objectives include continuing education, the establishment of a center for research and documentation, mutual support on issues affecting its members, coordination and concerned action on issues of the bigger society and recruitment of women theologians.[5]

Since then, these church women have come together for various activities. They have held breakfast fellowships which have as format: worship, common meal, an inspirational talk, a sharing of members attending international women's conferences, or a conference by visiting personalities. They have likewise come together in common studies in seminars and symposia. Noteworthy are the seminars on "Integral Evangelization and Structural Analysis" which sought to situate theologizing and the spreading of the good news in the context of the present Philippine situation. They have undertaken institutional analysis of each other's institutions, baring their strengths and weaknesses to one another and accepting suggestions and critique—all in the pursuit of a common goal: the transformation of society.

Not only were they together in common study, they have also found themselves working together among the urban poor, the political detainees and among factory workers.

Another common bond which has united church women is of course the cause of women as such. In the Philippines, we have the mistaken notion that "women do not need liberation because Filipino women are liberated." This is probably true for the middle class and upper class Filipino women who enjoy a lot of educational and economic privileges denied to many other Asian women. Yet statistically if one reflects on the fact that about 65% of Filipino women are in the rural areas, and about 20% belong to the urban poor then it is perhaps not quite right to say that Filipino women are liberated because 80-85% of them suffer some form of oppression—economic, political, sociocultural–and are deprived of the privileges enjoyed by the upper 20% of their sisters.

Taking cognizance of this fact, church women of varying denominations have come together in documenting oppression of women in various forms: prostitution, economic oppression of women textile workers, discriminating legal provisions, etc. One significant symposium held by the Path-Two on May 19-22, 1979, had as theme: Women's Issues in the Philippines. Outstanding women in their fields were invited to talk on burning issues such as Consumer Protection, Tourism and Prostitution, Urban and Rural Women Workers, the Nursing Profession, and Legal Rights of Women. At the end of the symposium the women came up with the following statement which I quote in full:

> We, the Philippine Association of Theologically Trained Women (PATH-TWO) representing nine churches, meeting in Consultation at Eliazo Hall,. Loyola Heights, Quezon City on May 19-22, 1979, have seriously deliberated on vital issues affecting Filipino women. In this consultation sponsored by the Asian Church Women Conference, the question was raised whether the Filipino woman is truly liberated. The consensus was that the upper and middle class Filipino woman is liberated. They enjoy certain privileges such as opportunities for education, employment, and leadership to a certain extent. However, they also are subject to discrimination both in the face of the law and actual life situations. This is due to age old conditioning and the conventional roles and status assigned to women by society. Furthermore, the greater percentage of Filipino women belonging to the lower classes are economically, politically, socially, and sexually exploited. They are also exploited and oppressed by structures of society and by men. They are also exploited and oppressed by other women belonging to the higher classes in society.

> The specific issues we focused on in our conference were: Consumer Issues and the Woman, Prostitution and Tourism, the Plight of Urban and Rural Women Workers, and Legal Rights of Women. Our insights are as follows:

Consumer Issues and the Filipino Women

> We have perceived the unabated rising prices of basic commodities due to the structure of our economic system, inflation, activities of transnational corporations, etc. At the same time we observe with dismay the lack of corresponding income increases to keep up with the price hike. We have likewise studied the many devious ways by which the consumer is deceived and shortchanged. The woman is most vitally affected by the issue because it is her task in Filipino society to see to it that the budget suffices for the needs of the family

*Of all women consumers, the most affected are those in
the low or no income groups.*

In relation to this,
- *we protest all unnecessary price hikes, taxes
  imposed taking advantage of the oil crisis;*
- *we deplore the lagging of wage increases behind
  the rate of price increases;*
- *we denounce all the devious ways by which the
  consumer is cheated and shortchanged;*
- *we affirm the need of consumers to organize to
  protect their rights as declared in the United
  Nations Declaration of Consumer Rights.*

Prostitution and Tourism

*We have seen how Tourism has made of prostitu-
tion a legalized, corporate institutionalized lucrative
enteprise in our country. The economic advantage that
is used to rationalise this is negligible and does not
justify the degradation and loss of dignity of the Filipino woman and of the erosion of values of our society
as a whole. We see that the problem of prostitution is
tied up with the basic economic problems and policies
in our country.*

In this connection,
- *we demand the cessation of sex tours that are
  freely advertised abroad as a basic part of our
  tourism program;*
- *we blame the lack of productive employment
  opportunities for Filipino women, especially of
  the low-income groups for the difficulty in solving
  the prostitution problem;*
- *we can tolerate tourism that is for genuine international understanding but never one which
  includes the degradaton of women.*

Women Workers: Urban and Rural

*Women workers suffer exploitation in their double
role as workers and housewives. As workers they are
discriminated in employment opportunities, in compensation, in terms and conditions of work. They are
also vulnerable to sexual exploitation from male super-
visors and employers. Among urban women workers,
we have singled out the problem of nurses who are*

underemployed in spite of the dire need of the country for health services especially in the rural areas. As a consequence they succumb to the brain drain and suffer oppression and exploitation when they go abroad. The rural women are the most oppressed of all, because they are subject to extreme poverty, ignorance, ill-health and maltreatment due to the prevailing feudal relationships in the family.

Relative to this,
- *we urge the Ministry of Health to fully and seriously implement the rural health program which should include a nurse in every barrio with adequate compensation;*
- *we support the formation of the union of women workers to fight for their basic rights;*
- *we realize the urgent need of education of rural women and join in the efforts at raising their consciousness.*

Legal Rights of Women

We are appalled by the knowledge that the Filipino woman is discriminated even under the law. And even when the law provides for equal treatment, such provisions are not implemented both in business and social life. This is caused by traditional biases against women in favor of men, by the economic climate that dictates that "Women are first fired, last hired," by the weakness of government machinery to enforce the law, as well as by the traditional attitude of many women about themselves. Furthermore laws are often made and interpreted by a male-dominated legislative judicial system.

In the light of these realities,

- *we fully support the revision of the laws discriminatory to women;*
- *we strongly urge the full implementation of laws that uphold equality of rights of women employees;*
- *we call for the demythologization of roles assigned to women by society;*
- *we rally all women to the cause of enhancing their self-image and building their —self-confidence.*

Conclusion

As theologically-trained women we have reflected on these realities in the light of our faith and of the Gospel message. And we are filled with a sense of urgency to join the struggle of our sisters in the different areas of conflict. We do not advocate a rivalry with men, but rather the release of the full potentials, common aspiration—that of societal transformation. We wish to share not only our insights but also this sense of urgency so that the time may soon come when—'there will be no differences between Jews and Gentiles, between slaves and free men, between men and women, for you all one in union with Christ Jesus." (Gal. 3:28 TEV) [6]

Members of the Path-Two have likewise represented the Philippines in various international conferences of women, for example in the Asian Church Women's Conference in India, in the Conference on Human Rights and Mission in Venice, sponsored by the Sub-unit on Women of the WCC, the International Conference of Women Pastors in the US, in the Women's Theological Consultation in Hongkong, etc. It is significant to mention that the Philippine delegate to the Catholic Women's Conference in India was the Protestant President of ACWC and the representative to the WCC-sponsored Venice Conference was a Catholic nun. In these international and local conferences among women of different denominations there is an atmosphere of total acceptance sometimes that each one belongs to another church. There is absolutely no embarassment or unease in participating in each other's worship or service. All are embued with the burning desire to liberate the manifold potentials of women into full development enabling then to participate creatively in the shaping of their world.

In 1983, the Path-Two changed its name to AWIT (Association of Women in Theology). Influenced by the growing women's consciousness and the initial efforts at feminist liberation theology, this ecumenical group of women have held seminars and lectures on women and religion.

In November, 1985, a Philippine delegation of Catholic and Protestant women joined other women of both denominations in the Continental Consultation sponsored by EATWOT (Ecumenical Association of Third World Theologians) on the theme: "Total Liberation from the Asian Point of View." Last December 1986, a similar ecumenical delegation attended the Continental Meeting of Women in Oaxtepec, Mexico where they shared with women from Africa and Latin America not only their respective situations but likewise their theological reflections on their situation and their strategies for change.   The genuine ecumenicity of the conference is reflected in its final document. We read:

> One of the notable features of his meeting was the atmosphere of serious study, sisterhood and friendliness which prevailed throughout. Worship times saw all the delegates praying together in the typical styles of each continent to the God of all nations. The themes (reality of oppression and struggle of women, vital aspects of women's experience of God in emerging spiritualities, woman and the Church, women and the Bible, women and Christology) were treated through presentations by skilled panelists for each of the three continents.[7]

Conclusion

In this reflection on the actual practice of ecumenism among church women, some insights confirm certain theses about ecumenism, namely:

1) Ecumenism will come about, less through theological discussions and more through praxis.

2) Ecumenical practice will not be realized through a descending movement from ecclesiastical authority to the rank and file but from people to legitimation by authority.

3) The realization of ecumenism will be through a common basis of unity which lies beyond the religious self-oriented interests of the churches. In the case of church women this common basis of unity is the solidarity with the struggle of the poor and the oppressed, especially of women. ☒

ENDNOTES

[1]Cf. August Kasler "Okumenische Bewegung" in Rahner (ed.) Herder Theologiches Taschen Lexicon, Vol. 5 (Freiburg: Herdes, 1973), pp. 249-254.

[2]Cf. Pedro S. Achutegui S.J., Ed., Ecumenism and Vatican II, Cardinal Bea Studies II, (Quezon City: Loyola School of Theology, 1972), and Achutegui

Towards a Dialogue of Life: Ecumenism in the Asian Context, Cardinal Bea Studies IV, (Quezon City: Loyola School of Theology, 1975).

[3]Andres Cristobal Cruz "Of Ecumenism Saecula-Saecolorum" in the Sunday Times Magazine, November 22, 1970, p. 20.

[4]Quoted in P.A. Zapanta, "Response to Ecumenism: Protestants Propose Togetherness" in Ibid., p. 36

[5]Rebecca Asedillo (ed.) Journal of the First Consultation of Theologically Trained Women, Mimeographed proceedings, p. 2

[6]"Statement on Women Issues of the Philippine Association of Theologically Trained Women."

[7]Final Document, Intercontinental Conference of Women, Oaxtepec, December, 1986.

ASIAN WOMEN DOING THEOLOGY

Myrna Francia, ICM, Roy Chiefe, O'Carm and Margaret Lacson

Gift and Challenge

Doing women's theology in Asia is a gift, a task and a challenge; writing about its dynamism and complexities is equally so, for women's theology in Asia is multi-faceted as well as unified. Writing about contextualized theology by Asian women is a gift for we were overwhelmed by the richness of God-experience of women dialoguing with Asian realities and cultures, deftly articulating the attitude of hope in the liberating Jesus from the perspective of faith in the Creating God, and the courageous active love of the Spirited women-communities. It is a task to understand and imagine its depth and promise, a struggle to break loose from preconceived notions inherited from the hellenized-roman world of meaning propagated by male masters and almost entirely internalized by women. Struggling free, we perceived woman no longer as thing but as light to see our present Asian as well as Philippine situation more lucidly. It gave us more reason to reflect theologically and to act. Finally, it is a challenge to present this wealth of insight, this warm light, coherently, faithfully and critically, and to foster its growth and acceptance in the male-dominated world of theology.

Yielding its Fruits

Usually, in a dynamic process which theologizing is intended to be, problems are elaborately presented and the solutions proposed are very thin. Hence, we would like to begin by presenting some first fruits yielded from feminist theology in Asia, namely, new imagery, new art, new liturgy.

India's Lucy d'Souza creatively presented woman as a

---

*A paper presented to Dr. Jose de Mesa's Fundamental Theology class at the Maryhill School of Theology.

mango tree, [1] growing, nurturing, giving, and yet in danger of being wantonly cut down. The painting relates the oppression of women to the crime of deforestation. At the same time, the woman stands quietly with arms spread out in a gesture of giving and accepting. Tree is a traditional symbol of life in Indian culture and in Christian tradition, it is life-giving because Jesus died on it in the form of a cross. Intuitively, the artist redeems woman's sufferings by making it creative in the dimension of resurrection. For us, this art-work illustrates Psalm 1:

> The righteous (woman) is a tree
> planted by streams of water
> yielding its fruits in its season
> and its leaf does not wither.

Aruna Granadason's liturgy, "A Mother Turned Woman", [2] grips us in its rootedness in the stark reality of India's history of anti-woman practices such as dowry and suttee (bride burning). The courageous reaction of the mother-turned-woman reflects many Asian women's insight regarding the encounter of women with the Bible. With her life-blood flowing out, and her back bent from such discriminations, woman looks to Jesus and hears his word of life, suddenly she gains courage to stand upright. From the life-less ashes of her daughter springs new life for the mother:

> O daughter of mine, I love you
> for a woman you have made me.
> No longer will I remain entombed in silence.
> No longer will my daughter or any other daughter burn.
> I thank you for teaching me
> the power of womanhood.

The Intercessory Prayer asks forgiveness for "hiding our faces behind our privileged positions, our institutions, our theology." Repentance then becomes a condition for doing authentic women's theology, a diversion from a pattern of domination of women. Rev. Sun Ai Park (Korea) deepens the significance of repentance within a patriarchal context: "The man who accepts the other who comes to him in the form of his wife is saved from his partaking of the sin of the patriarchal system as a man." [3]

In Korea, women participate actively in minjung theology by listening to and eliminating *han* which is the people's historically unresolved and accumulated frustration and resentment. *Han* is the cry of the little people, in Tagalog it is the collective *hinanaing*, in Hebrew, *za'ak* (Ex 3:7). Women point out one experience of this cry or *hinanaing*: rape.

Sun Ai relates the story of a militant student who was raped during detention and who afterwards made the radical decision to speak out and denounce her police-violators. Sun Ai reflects: "for the love of justice, this woman denied herself completely, took courage to make public her deepest shame. Is this not the grain of wheat which falls and dies, that new grains may sprout?"[4]   When many more silenced voices speak out, this cross of humiliation will be a vindication. A rich harvest of justice can be reaped only if violated women themselves dare to rise above their shame and hence wield power in their powerlessness.

From the gut experience of a mother losing her only daugther to cancer, Ahn Sang Nim, a Korean mother-theologian, re-discovered the mother image of God, which had long been forgotten in the Judeo-Christian Tradition (JCT) of God-the-Father. From the depths of pain and loss, she cried out, "My God, what are you?" A vague philosophical 'Being Itself' who remains deaf to a mother's cry? A king basking in imperial glory? A strict father who punishes wrong-doings? Rejecting these patriarchal images, she sought consolation in the Bible. "The mother image of God in the Bible made me feel closer to God, helped me to understand God's will more easily. God's love, which I could not feel when I imagined God as father, became clearer when I compare it with my feelings toward my children... When I was crying over my daughter, God also cried. I don't think God punished me." [5]   From her experience as mother, she could attribute to God-the-Mother feelings of pain when her children fight with each other anger upon seeing even one life hurt and violated, sadness when people destroy creation. "Oh, how God must weep over this troubled world."

Patriarchal Connection

A male author, Multatuli, gave this tale:

Once upon a time, there lived a girl and her three brothers. Together they had the task of milking their father's cows. There came a day when the brothers became unhappy with their life and desired to seek other opportunities for self-development. They wanted to live their own lives, satisfying their own needs. Off to their father they went to tell of their desire. But father refused to let them go for who would tend the cows? "Let our sister do it," they said. "But what if she wants to live her own life too?" father asked. They replied, "Please father, don't teach her anything." But father argued further, "Perhaps she will still get to think that life has more to offer her." The brothers then advised their father, "Father, why don't you tell her that it is a sin for a girl to think, to understand, and to desire?" "That's not a bad idea," agreed the father. So the sons left and travelled the whole world running after their dreams. But sister stayed home. And that is how it is until this day. 6

Multatuli's tale — truth or fiction? Biblical research by women theologicans underscore the truth of male exploitation in the story as experienced by women in the Judaic society. Most women, including our Asian theologians, would accept the truth of the story based on their actual experiences of male domination and oppression, not only in society but in the Church as well. A constant theme explicitly tackled by all women doing theology is patriarchy.

A raw nerve was exposed when feminist movements penetrated the aching tooth (too much sweet life?) of capitalism. New Testament scholar, Sandra Schneiders, radically summarizes this discovery:

Patriarchy is the basic principle underlying not only the subordination of women to men, but of one race to another, of colonies to master nations, of children to adults, of nations to divine right monarchs, of believers to clergy. In other words, patriarchy is the nerve of racism, classism, colonialism and clericalism as well as of sexism. Fundamentally, patriarchy is a masculine power structure in which all relationships are understood in terms of superiority and inferiority, and social cohesion is assured by the exercise of dominative power. 7

The subjugation of women keeps these patriarchal structures intact; therefore, women doing theology recognize their urgent task of unmasking the patriarchal connections in culture and theology. Feminist theology sustains an ideological suspicion of systems and values stemming from patriarchy. In this sense, feminist theology could be called a subversive theology for it upsets the accepted dominance of masculinity in all areas of life including religion.

Reformulation of theologies in the Third World then can only be truly relevant if they contain the perspective and the contribution of its women. No theology of liberation can be authentically liberating and liberated until the patriarchal structures predicated upon sexual inequality is addressed by its women through committed action for change. To be true to its liberation, theology requires a feminist hermeneutic since the patriarchal bias of the Bible has imprisoned the full life-giving message of the Word of God. In other words, a new approach and insight from the feminist perspective is required in order to release the message of life and love into its fuller meaning, i.e. the feminine dimension. However, we hasten to add that there is no fullest sense on this side of heaven because of the eschatological character of God's revelation. (We were tempted to add a naughty remark: would even God not have been tempted to reveal the whole of Himself under pressure of attractive women's wiles? — until we chided ourselves, certain that we fell captive to the male's dominant trend of thinking and joking!)

Hermeneutics of Asian Feminist Theology

Women's contextual theology in Asia is a conscious and systematic effort to understand God's offer of life and love from the perspective of Asian women's experience of economic exploitation and cultural oppression within patriarchal structures. It is the "irruption" [8] of women into history and theology, even into the theology of liberation, as the primary subject of liberation from their humiliated status towards fuller humanity.

To acquire an expanded self-understanding as Asian women-disciples of Christ, the Asian women theologians engaged in a dialectical hermeneutic between the biblical tradition and their contemporary women's situation. In our examples, we deal particularly with Korean and Filipino situations. The very text of Scriptures constitutes the product of tradition, that is, the manner in which the primitive church understood, interpreted, and committed to writing the original words and deeds of Jesus. Today we continue to invoke the hermeneutical principle, according to "which the philosophical context (or existential context) from which the formulation of a truth of faith is derived may be expendable and replaceable. This means that in a changed scientific and philosophical situation, a truth of faith calls for new interpretations and formulation, hence grasped in a new light." 9

Whereas in the past, development of meaningful religious signification was done from a mainly philosophical context, i.e. the Greco-Roman worldview, today, truth of faith can be interpreted not from philosophical concepts primarily but from a sociological-anthropological framework. This interpretative grid seems to be a valid attempt to understand God's continuing offer of life and love, so long as it is done in an attitude of "creative fidelity based on the identity of the Christ of glory with the historical Jesus." 10

In this dialectical hermeneutic, both biblical tradition and contemporary situation serve as 'source' and 'target' 11 for mutual affirmation and critique. For instance, what challenges or insights can the biblical tradition throw in the Korean woman's experiences of pain and oppression? On the other hand, does our economic-political analysis and/or cultural discernment of present systems uncover aspects of the biblical tradition as yet hidden through layers of male Greek philosophical traditioning? Let us see how this is applied in two instances: the Korean mother's experience and the Filipino women's struggle.

The Korean Experience

1. The starting term is the mother's, *hic et nunc*, namely, anguish due to the loss of her only child, and her rejection of the guilt feelings attributed to her by outsiders. God's traditional answers punished her for being too happy or not praying hard enough. For her, this painful experience becomes the locus of revelation of God-the-Mother.

2. Taking up the Bible as her source of light and strength, she discovers the mother-images of God, e.g. Jer 31:20:

> My womb trembles for my child
> I will truly show my motherly
> compassion upon him.

This tender mother-image became then the stern critic of one Korean cultural explanation of this death, i.e. "you are too happy so God used this way to teach you about his world." The wheel of fortune belief is dismissed by the active concern of the mother-God. The persevering nurturing concern of God-the-Mother does not submit to the avenging God who was accused of victimizing the daughter for the parents' lack of religiosity.

3. Her gut experience as mother, recalling her own tender feelings towards her daughter, is her source of light which unmasks the almost exclusive male-image of God in the Bible which has been emphasized throughout the ages of patriarchal-dominant interpretation. Theological affirmations couched in foreign philosophical concepts addressed to the intellect give way to affirmations in psychological concepts addressed to the imagination. Not only was the intelligibility of God's reality illumined but a contemplative gaze into God's desirability was allowed.

4. Knowing God's will from the deep experience of a mother's love led to an effective revelation of God as the Loving One, with a mother's plan of life and love for all Her children. God-Mother becomes the basis for ethical demands, an impetus for transforming action by women.

5. A program of action is discovered:

> a. women are prime movers of anti-nuclear movements because they are life-nurturing
> b. women nurture all of creation; hence, ecological action, care for the weak, simple life-style
> c. a spirituality, no longer of resignation, but of struggle against bondage which prevents the reign of God

There is a radical transformation in this mother — from an anguished concern for her dying daughter to an urgent concern for the dying earth.

The Philippine Experience

1. Reflecting on the sufferings and responses of countless Filipinos under the yoke of the dominant system of capitalism-militarism, our Filipina theologian recovers the Christ Event and points to two moments of Jesus' passion:-

> 1.1. the moment of undergoing "powerlessness before the collusion of civic-religious leaders in the Roman-dominated society of his time; physical suffering and humiliation"
> 1.2. the moment of accompanying and doing

In the mountains of Kalinga-Apayao, the women and

their families were threatened with innundation of their ancestral lands to make way for the 'god of progress' in the Chico river dam. Refusing to accept destruction of their barrios, displacement of their families, and rejecting empty promises, the bare-breasted Kalinga women dismantled the military camp with determined action and success.

Exploring the history of women's sufferings and humiliation sheds light on the radical depth of the Suffering Servant's humiliations (Isaiah) as solidarity and identification with womankind.

2. "Christ's passion as an act of solidarity with his people is alive among the militant, protesting Filipino women who have taken up the cudgels of the struggle for themselves and for the rest of the Filipino nation," becomes her re-reading of the historical event come alive in 1985.

But Jesus' solidarity was already revealed in his initial act of accompaniment -- the Incarnation -- carried through in his teaching and healing, a life of protest addressed to the powers that be. His passion was only a continuation of this accompaniment.

The weeping of the women of Jerusalem is no longer seen as a sentimental emotional but as a daring political act whereby the women, in their compassion, take a stand beside a politically condemned man, heedless of the threatening system.

From a politically-committed stance among militant Christian women, the historical Jesus and his companions become politically colored. Water of tears can be turned into the blood of martyrdom, i.e. Filipinas who accompany their suffering brothers unto torture and death.

3. This fresh political-materialist reading of Jesus' passion gives impetus for mission today: "the passion of Christ in the Filipino people is fashioning women disciples who could accompany the suffering Christ alive among the people." This Filipina theologian affirms a renewed spirituality — readiness to console and support as well as to die with the people. Death takes on a new level of meaning.

Evaluation

Strong Points

1. Women affirm themselves as subjects and primary objects of their theological affirmations.
2. AWDT uses scientific tools of analysis and hermeneutics.
3. AWDT uses inclusive language, is open to partnership with men towards renewed humanity and creation.
4. AWDT goes beyond individual theological reflection, into teamwork: consultation, composite papers.
5. AWDT has drawn a concrete action program.

Weak Points

1. AWDT deals with schematic, sporadic, reflections on issues or questions experienced rather than whole systematic theology.
2. Assumptions and pre-suppositions about AWDT's epistemology need to be spelled out and limitations need to be defined.
3. Some persons is strong on Marxist tools of analysis, but weak on societal cultural-religious analysis.
4. AWDT does not clarify to the extent of Marxist appropriations on theology.
5. Some persons think that the value of the real practice of the faith community does not surface, hence the impresson one gets is that of an intellectual middle class talking for the community instead of dialoguing with them. [12]

AWDT is responding to a felt need. It undergoes a courageous process with a sense of urgency having been faced with layers of structural and cultural problems intertwined in society and theology. Its endeavors are not isolated probings or anguished questioning but communication among individuals and groups. Different groups from each country inspire and mutually contaminate creative enthusiasm for further and deeper output.

While the women theologians share similar elements in their methodology, it cannot be concluded that these elements are equally stressed in every country. The countries in Asia would demand more probing of their cultural-religious heritage whereas the Marxist tools of economic-political analysis seem to be taken for granted as helpful. Existential reflection may remain on the analytical level and there may not be enough emphasis on the religious significance for the community of believers. A challenge to feminist theology in Asia is not to remain on the polemics of women's liberation nor read every experience with visionary eyes for justice and peace, but to develop a whole theology (pastoral, moral sacramental, systematic) from the new perspective of the feminine. The field is open. Shall men join the game fairly?

Reflections from Liberated Men

Excerpt from a poem "Darning a bed sheet" by a Korean factory worker, Mr. Park No-Hai

As much as the workers are not
productive machines of profit
my wife is not my handmaid
Husband and wife are loving friends
of equal stand
whose relationship is founded
on trust, respect
and democratic sharing

Dr. Joe de Mesa in his chalktalk

One of Dr. de Mesa's articulation of theology is his chalktalk. He uses the figure of woman not to portray temptresses, leading men to sin. On the contrary, the women figures he portrays are leading men to new insights and new experiences.

Roy, our groupmate

As a man, it is my pleasure to be part of the group which tackled the topic, "Asian women's perspective on theologizing." Every meeting, I learned new things which I felt were liberating. I was excited to participate and to seriously learn from women.

What had struck me most in my reading and in our sharing is the claim that in liberating themselves, the women actually help to liberate the men as well, the ultimate vision is that female and male must be equal. Therefore, their task is to work hand in hand in building the reign of God on earth here and now.

I am not hesitant to say that I feel I am in the process of liberating myself from the oppressive condition which we have been perpetuating, i.e. the superiority of male over female. Only when men can participate in women's struggle can men say that they are faithful to God. ஐ

ENDNOTES

[1]Cover of In God's Image (Asian women's theological journal). April 1985.

[2]Proceedings of Asian Women's Consultation (AWC) held in Manila, on November 21-30, 1985.

[3]Sun Ai Park. In God's Image. August 1985.

[4]Ibid.

[5]Proceedings, AWC

[6]As translated from a magazine. Tijdschright voor Geestelijk Leven. August 1987.

[7]Sandra Schneiders. *Women and the World.* (New York: Paulist Press, 1986).

[8]Virginia Fabella and Sergio Torres. *Irruption of the Third World* (Maryknoll: Orbis Books, 1983) p. xii

Virginia Fabella and Sergio Torres, *Doing Theology in a Divided World* (Maryknowll: Orbis Books, 1985), p. 209.

[9]Gutwanger in *Sacramentum Mundi*, No. 6 p. 293.

[10]Clodovis Boff, *Theology and Praxis*, Epistemological Foundation (Maryknoll: Orbis Books, 1987), p. 149.

[11]Joe de Mesa, "Inculturation", *Kerygma* 20, 1986, pp. 166-167.

[12]Proceedings, AWC.

TOWARDS AN ASIAN FEMINIST THEOLOGY

Sr. Mary John Mananzan, OSB

Introduction

In several Asian countries there has been an emerging consciousness among Catholic and Protestant women of the need to theologically reflect on the situation of women and their on-going struggles. They also find the necessity of re-thinking, re-interpreting and re-formulating biblical and theological concepts, and of evolving a spirituality from the point of view of third world women in Asia.

This contribution will be historical in approach-tracing the efforts of Asian women to develop an Asian feminist theology, but it will likewise be descriptive of the results of these efforts both in content and method. It will be divided into 6 main sections;

1. Initial Efforts before the Geneva Conference in 1982
2. The Birth of EATWOT Commission on Women
3. National Consultations in Different Asian Countries
4. The Asian Continental Women's Consultation
5. Methodology and Significant Insights of Asian Women's Theology
6. Future Perspective

Initial Efforts of Asian Women

Feminist theology is relatively a new venture in Asia. In the 70s there were some initial efforts at convoking consultations of church women. Associations of theologically trained women were formed in several countries. However, these were more concerned with the study programs, status, work conditions and participation in the church of these women rather than in actually theologizing from the point of view of Asian women.

In the Philippines, an Association called PATH-TWO (Philippine Association of Theologically Trained Women) was established at the closing of the first consultation of Theologically Trained Women held in the Philippines from June 6-8, 1978. The consultation had as theme "Church Women: Speak, Lead and Share." The PATH-TWO tackled issues on women like the prostitution question, and successfully campaigned against the Japanese sex tours. It also sponsored seminars on the interpretation of the Bible from women's point of view.

A Women's Desk was established by the Christian Conference of Asia in 1980 which launched Asian consultation regarding women issues in the region. A lot of reflection and lectures on religion and women's issues were conducted but the formal, conscious and directed development of a feminist theology from the Asian Women's point of view was not undertaken. It took the EATWOT First World-Third World Theologian's Dialogue to launch such a project in Geneva last January, 1982.

Birth of the EATWOT Commission on Women

On January 1983 EATWOT (Ecumenical Association of Third World Theologians) held a dialogue between Third World Theologians with their First World counterparts. About 1/3 of the delegates to the Geneva Conference were women. They met among themselves, clarified their orientations to each other and modified the agenda of the conference to include a forum on women. A resolution made in that conference was to establish a Women's Desk that has the specific purpose of developing a theology of liberation from the point of view of third world women. It formulated its tasks as follows:

1. To make a structural analysis of the situation of women: economic, political, socio-cultural and religous.
2. To discuss the patriarchal element in Theology today.
3. To reformulate theology from the perspective of a full humanity.

The Ad Hoc Committee that worked out the program in Geneva listed the following themes as subject matter of the reflections of the Women Theologians in developing a feminist liberation theology for the perspective of the Third World:

1. Various oppression of women and women's responses in
   a) society
   b) church
2. Social analysis of their respective country
   a) economic structure
   b) political
   c) socio-cultural-religious situations
3. Theological reflection
   a) Hermeneutical analysis
      -- of the Bible
      -- of other sources such as myths, folklore, legends, indigenous religions
   b) Reflection on
      -- God-talk and woman
      -- Christology and woman
      -- Mariology and woman
      -- Pneutology and woman
4. Emerging Forms of spirituality

The process deemed most conducive to the realization of the project was to hold various conferences:

a) National Consultations—where women interested in Theology will dialogue with grassroots women in their country to reflect in faith about the situations of women in the respective countries.

b) Continental Conferences — where women of the different countries come together to share their theological reflections.

c) Intercontinental Fellowship—where the women from Asia, Africa and Latin America reflect on the differences and commonalities of their theological reflection and methodologies.

d) First World-Third World Women Theologians' Dialogue — the culminating activity where the Third World women theologians and the first world women theologians share their contributions towards the development of a feminist theology of liberation.

National Consultation of Feminist Theology in Asia

Faithful to the mandate of the Geneva resolution approved on January 15, 1983 by the EATWOT Executive

Committee, the assigned Asian Coordinator Sun Ai Park established national contacts with the different countries of Asia--writing letters and visiting different Asian countries to promote the coming together of women theologians to initiate theological reflection from the point of view of women. The response was enthusiastic.

First, the Korean Association of Women Theologians (KAWT) held two consultations on the initiation of feminist theology. The first was held in 1983. It addressed the academe and professional theologians focusing itself on Korean history and tradition.[2] The second consultation was held in 1984 and had as its theme "The Milieu of Korean Feminist Theology." This time the focus was on the current Korean situation especially on the areas of labour, farmers, and urban poor. It had as sub-theme "Sex Exploitation and the situation of Korean women Living Outside Korea." From the evaluation of this consultation we read:

> As a result of this consultation, Feminist Theology and Minjung Theology have become closer. The Korean Centre for Theological Studies invited representatives of KAWT to meet the Minjung Theologians for a discussion of the seminar.

> Another result was the interest in KAWT by groups unrelated with it. People involved in the human rights movement and movement for the poor have been drawn closer. KAWT and Feminist Theology formed a connection because of the consultation.[3]

Second, last November 21-24, 1984, the All Indian Council of Christian Women held a national consultation with theme "Towards a Theology of Humanhood: Women's Perspective." The purpose of the dialogue was for Indian women "to join the Biblical dialogue so as to reconstruct women's early Christian history." It formulated as one of its objectives the adoption of a feminist model which provided a theological understanding of one's faith based on the experience of Indian women rooted in their present socio-economic context. At the same time, another attempt to initiate a feminist theology in India was undertaken by Ishvani Kendra in coordination with Pro Mundi Vita.

A draft of a course description that was adopted by the project had as its aim: "provide participants the opportunity to discuss some research and writings on the development of a theology from a feminist perspective and to contribute to that enterprise from Indian women's experience and in an Indian way."4

In the Philippines, women's organization have come to bloom in the '80s. Since the most important of these organizations began as militant women's organization in the political struggle, there was a need to clarify the distinctly feminist perspective. Women have their own problems and interests even if the women's movement in the third world need to locate the liberation of woman in the economic, political and socio-cultural liberation of society as a whole. This condition is necessary though not sufficient for the liberation of women.

It is in the context of this ferment that the Filipino women engaged in theology located their National Consultation on December 22-29, 1984. The Consultation pinpointed as objective the promotion of a theology of struggle from the perspective of women in the third world. Moreover it aimed at helping to fulfill the aspirations of the poor Filipinos for total national liberation with a focus on women's struggle through theology.

In one of the reflections, the women declared that "the Filipino women's struggle for equality and liberation is multidimensional. It starts from a realization of being oppressed." Furthermore, "women need to be united in order to reclaim their rightful place in the order of creation and be empowered to liberate themselves."5

Also, Hongkong held its consultation last August 26, 1985 with its theme "Men and Women Are One in Christ". It had two objectives: the first was to explore the development of the feminist theology in Hongkong; the second was to draw inspiration from women's living experiences as the basis of theological reflection.6

In the discussions some directions came up for the future development of feminist theologizing. Among these were:

-- Feminist Theology, unlike traditional theology, emphasized women's experiences as starting point of theological reflection.
-- The mandate of feminist theology is to restore an inclusive full humanity approach in contrast to a male-centered one.

-- Feminist theology emphasizes mutual relationship rather than hierarchy.
-- Feminist theology is founded on historical tradition.
-- Feminist theology seeks to find a relevant contextualized theology for men and women today.
-- There cannot be only *one* feminist theology[7]

The Consultation pointed out the necessity of using folklore, myth, and legends of the Chinese tradition as further sources of theological reflection on Chinese women. It also deplored the still predominantly middle-class character of feminist theology today.

Lastly, in the October 1985 Malaysian consultation, a parallelism was drawn between the social realities of Israel and Palestine and the present Malaysian society particularly the New Economic Policy (NEP) which they contrasted to the concept of the Jewish Jubilee Year. The difference lies in the NEP's implementation which is only "good news" to a few but "bad news" to the greater majority of Malaysians. It has in fact given rise to racial tension and greater gap between the rich and the poor. The consultation concluded: "women doing theology from the Asian perspective is a new phenomenon in the history of the Church in Malaysia. A small grain of mustard seed is taking root and sprouting in the hands of many. We pray for greater faith, hope and courage to move forward in the spirit."[8]

The Asian Continental Consultation

After the National Consultations, a Continental conference was held on November 21-30, 1985. Twenty-seven Church women from Hongkong, India, Japan, Korea, Malaysia, Sri-Lanka and the Philippines met in Manila to share their insights and theological reflections on Total Liberation from the Perspectives of Asian Women. This was the culmination of the preparatory discussions in the different countries.

The consultation process consisted of exposures to urban and rural areas, national reports, biblical reflections, national situationers, creative liturgical celebration and theological reflections on the following topics:

-- Women's Oppression, a Sinful Situation
-- God-talk and Women
-- Women and the Christ Event

-- Women and the Faith Community
-- Women and Mary
-- Women and the Holy Spirit

This consultation was significant because it introduced women into the working methodology of feminist theology. It meant contextualizing the reflection in concrete situations of women in the different countries. It meant the initiation into the unaccustomed collective effort at making composite papers. It called for the creation of original methods like the mural painting done by the women which evoked the artistic expression of insights on women and their situation. The physical arrangement of having cushions and mattresses on the floor where the women could relax in various positions during the plenum created an atmosphere conducive to free-flowing and in-depth sharing.

The women denounced the oppression and dehumanization in various forms of their Asian sisters stemming from economic exploitation, foreign domination, state repression, militarization and racial strife. These are manifested in different ways in different countries:

-- In India, through the dowry system, bride burning, forced sterilization and sex discrimination.
-- In the Philippines, through job discrimination, exposure to health hazards in factories, institutional prostitution due to sex tourism, torture and rape in military interrogations.
-- In Malaysia, through resurgence of religious fundamentalism, worsening communal relation and diminishing political freedom.
-- In Japan, through the continuance of the male-oriented emperor system and the development of highly dangerous technology with its concommitant deadly hazards to health.
-- In Korea, through the painful separation felt because of the division of their homeland, the growing militarism and the continuous grip of Confucian family law which makes the male the absolute master in all aspects of life.

The delegates also realized that the highly patriarchal churches in their countries definitely contributed to the subjugation and marginalization of women. In fact theology itself has added to the distortions. We read:

We unearthed theological premises, traditions, and beliefs that have prevented us from becoming fully human and have blurred the image of God that we are. These elements are:

-- *the patriarchal image we have of God;*
-- *the predominance of male interpretations of the Bible;*
-- *the emphasis on the maleness of Jesus which has been used to discriminate against women in the church and society;*
-- *the propagation of a "Mary Cult" which has not only violated the person of Mary but also dislocated her and minimized her active role in salvation history; and*
-- *the bias against women in Christian tradition buttressed the male-oriented Asian religious belief.*[9]

Methodology and Significant Insights in Asian Women Theology

As has been stated before, theologizing from the Asian women's point of view is a very new endeavor. It is an ongoing process. However, the last four years that followed the establishment of EATWOT Women's Commission can show an emerging methodology and significant insights that can already be shared.

The emerging features of feminist theology are the following:

1. *Contextualization* - The starting point is the experience of Asian women and their struggle in a male dominated world. Women tell their stories consciously and politically and in this act they begin to understand themselves and their reality better.

2) *Religious and Cultural Critique* - The insight that all religions and cultures contain both liberating and oppressive forces urges the necessity of a critique of religion and culture identifying the elements that legitimate and perpetuate the oppression and domination of women.

3) *Recovery of the authentic value of Women's Experience* - Women recognize their religious heritage while rejecting an imposed tradition. Women realize that their spiritual tradition goes beyond the official context of religion and theology.

4) *Reinterpretation and Re-formulation* - As women bring into their religious tradition the questions and deep concerns that arise out of the inexperience and analysis of their social context, new translations, new interpretations, new language emerge. Religious insights are expressed in a vast array of religious forms. Women's experiences create religious symbols and stories which contribute to the development of a faith-filled response to the historical moment.

5) *New Visions* - Women envision new possibilities for community and they struggle to realize these possibilities. It is the struggle that gives power, strength, hope and concreteness to these new visions. In turn, it is the vision that gives direction to women's struggles. It is through political action for social transformation that women's theologizing is verified.[10]

The preceding elements can be used all over the world. In Asia, the home of the great oriental religions which strongly permeate Asian culture, there is a need for culture and religion to be more thoroughly analyzed and studied, as they affect women often legitimizing their domination and oppression. The fact that in almost all Asian countries Christianity was used to subjugate peoples and was introduced through colonization, necessitates a critique of this type of colonial Christianity in theologizing from the Asian women's point of view. At the same time the rich cultural heritage, the varied and oral tradition, myths, legends, folklore that abound in Asia, that mirror Asian society through the years provide Asian women additional sources, aside from the Scriptures, for understanding themselves.

Finally, the presence of militant struggles against fascism and imperialism in many Asian countries provide the crucible that put the faith of Asians to the test, giving them a sense of urgency in rethinking and reformulating the different aspects of their faith and religious values.

The Oaxtepec Encounter

On December 2-6, 1986, 8 women from different countries of Asia met with women from Africa and Latin America in an intercontinental conference held in Oaxtepec, Mexico. The theme of the conference was "Doing Theology from the Third World Women's Perspective." Commonalities and differences in doing theology were discussed. They came out with 4 main insights, namely:

1. The oppression of women in the three continents is a hard and abiding reality in all spheres of life: economic, social, political, cultural, social, sexual and religious.

2. In all the three continents, the women have organized themselves to struggle for their right. Some of these movements are motivated by Christian faith. Among the efforts made towards liberation from oppression, theologizing emerges as a specific move by which women struggle for their right to life.

3. The Bible plays a vital role in the lives of women and in their struggle for liberation. Instead of rejecting the Bible wholesale because of its patriarchal aspects the participants felt the need of delving deeper into it, rejecting the patriarchal crust and highlighting the neglected elements which portray women as individuals in their own right and as God's co-workers and agents of life.

4. In all three continents women constitute a vital and dynamic force within the Church. There is an urgent need to discover new ways of seeing the world as the visible presence of God's kingdom, and of the New Creation.[11]

Future Prospects

The seed has been sown in several Asian countries. A momentum has been started and structures have been set for the continuing theological reflection from the point of view of Asian women. The encounter with the women of the other two continents have given a further impetus to the task.

In December 1987, an Asian Consultation will be held in Singapore to share the insights gained in the previous conferences to other Asian women interested in doing theology from the perspective of Third World Women.

In 1988 a dialogue will be held between Third World Women representatives from the three continents and women theologians from cultural minorities in first world countries.

In 1989 an encounter is planned between representatives of the Third World Women and their Sisters in the First World.

Conclusion

A call to commitment and action by the women in the Asian Women Consultation:

We Asian churchwomen, declare our strong solidarity with the oppressed people—the worker, the farmers, the fisherfolk, the urban poor, the tribal and ethnic minorities, and most especially the women—in the painful struggle for full humanity.

We denounce foreign domination, state repression, militarism, dehumanizing capitalism and all forms of evil that subjugate women.

We offer our collective strength and power to our Asian sisters in the fight against poverty and oppression.

We staunchly support women's movements in confronting patriarchal structures and traditions; we are one in struggling for democratization in the home, the Church, the schools, and society in general.

We will constantly exercise vigilance in upholding women's rights to equality and self-determination; we will work unceasingly to lift our suffering sisters—the battered, the tortured, the hungry, the silenced and the unfree.

We firmly resolve to promote authentic feminist education and the development of a liberating theology from the perspective of Asian women.

We strongly encourage new forms and ways of communication that will make us aware of issues that affect our lives and our futures.

We reach out and join hands with our sisters beyond our shores. Together we will rise from our bondage and heal our wounds; together we will continue to hold up half the sky and move mountains.

We call for unity and solidarity, for it is only by working together towards a new community of women and men will the world witness the coming of the new kingdom which is the embodiment of justice, equality, peace and love.[12]

END NOTES

[1]Project Proposal of the EATWOT Commission on Women, Geneva, January 1982.

[2]General Comment on the 2nd Consultation for the establishment of Feminist Theology in Asia by Rev. Chung Sook Ja, KAWT, General Secretary.

[3]Ibid. p. 4.

[4]Program Invitation to the Indian National Consultation.

[5]From the proceedings of the Tagaytay Consultation.

[6]From the Report of the Hongkong National Consultation.

[7]Loc. Cit.

[8]Malaysian National Consultation report.

[9]From the "Asian Church Women Speak." The Final Statement of the Asian Consultation of Women in Voices. Vol. 8, No. 2, Dec. 1985 p. 34.

[10]"How to" Skill Pocket put out by Church Women United.

[11]From the final document of the Intercontinental Women's Conference in Oaxtepec Mexico, Dec. 2-6, 1986.

[12]Voices From the Third World, Phil. Ed., Vol. III, No. 2, Dec. 1985, p. 35-36.

oppression

and

liberation

Sr. Mary Kristia Bacani, OSB

It is useless to cherish "ideals" which, as we imagine will help us to escape from a self with which we are dissatisfied or disgusted. The way of perfection is not a way of escape. We can only become saints by facing ourselves, by assuming full responsibility for our lives just as they are, with all their handicaps and limitations, and submitting ourselves to the purifying and transforming action of the Savior.

Thomas Merton

The early events of my life were full of peculiar experiences: I came from a mixed marriage — my mother, a staunch Methodist Protestant, my father, a critical and questioning Roman Catholic, and what more, my paternal grandmother was a very devout Roman Catholic married to a steadfast Aglipayan.

This startling array of relationships made it easy and yet difficult for me to decide to whom I will give my innocent allegiance then. My parents' preoccupation with their own professional growth and training decided it all for me: I had to stay and grow up with my paternal grandparents.

I remember my first notion of God at age five: GOD was a woman and her name was Mary, and Mary was with child. My Lola (grandmother) called her Mother of Perpetual Help. Every Wednesday, we got up early to be in her Baclaran shrine. I recall that the only thing that made me wake up early and be with my Lola was the promise of rice cakes, chocolate candies, balloons, colorful sparrows and painted clay toys. My Lola had varied views regarding Mama Mary: she is a refuge to those in danger; she drives away all evil, especially Satan who wishes to take everyone along to a fiery place...

where people's blood is sucked for monetary production; make a novena (nine-day prayer) to her and she will grant you your heart's desire, more so if you walk on your knees towards her altar!

Later on, I realized that Mother Mary is not only found in Baclaran, but also in our very own Parish Church, but her name is Virgin of Lourdes or Lady of Loreto, Virgin of Sorrows, Our Lady of Fatima or our Lady of Mount Carmel! I also became acquainted with her numerous holy-looking friends like Saint Therese of the Child Jesus, Saint Rita of Casia, Saint Anthony of Padua, Saint Jude and Saint Roque and many more. As I glance at their images from the many plaster statues in the church and at my Lola's pile of novena booklets, I also learned that each of them had a special line of assistance: a saint for those in need of a husband, one for finding a lost item, another for a safe trip, still another for a successful examination and many more!

Lola also taught me how to make the sign of the cross by myself. I asked her why Mother Mary was not in that "prayer," she smiled and shrugged off her answer. My first effort to question was aborted after that, until my first summer vacation with my mother at age 7. She took me to Sunday School where I met children singing "Jesus is a Happy Name." I asked my mother, "Who is Jesus?" My mother's prompt answer was, "He is God, our good shepherd!" "I thought God's name was Mary!?" I said. She led me to a Bible where the full story of Jesus is written. Enthusiastically, I shared such an experience with Lola, only to be admonished that I should never read the Bible as it is the book of Protestants. I took her advice and again, my questioning was put off. Period.

I studied in public non-sectarian schools all my life. But before I received first communion at age nine, I was under the mentorship of a religion teacher from our parish. She required us to do so much memory work not only confined to prayers but also to gestures: how to kneel, how to approach the altar, how to genuflect and how to open one's mouth in receiving the body of Jesus. Several times a day, she would repeat reminders on the type of shoes, dress, veil to wear. She sounded like a quack doctor detailedly describing what to bring and what not to bring in order to have a successful rite of exorcism.

To top it all, she left me a remarkable notion of God: He

was an old man who sees everything I do, say and think. He throws all those who disobey Him to hell! Alas! God was not a woman nor a good shepherd. He was a strict policeman who runs after bad and wicked people.

I remember all these in fear... I had no alternative but to obey, yes, to obey unquestioningly! This led me to acquire scruples about my fear of God. My teenage life was ushered in by more dedicated novenas and devotions. Lola required me to wear some religious garb and articles: the blue sash of the Lady of Lourdes on Saturdays and the red sash of the Holy Infant Jesus on Sundays, aside from the scapulars of the Sacred Heart of Jesus and the Lady of Mount Carmel.

The first sixteen years of my life was a time of passivity and submissiveness, expressed in an ambience of domestic religiosity and family dominance. My mind was conditioned to believe that the ideal woman was unsophisticated, innocent, passive, young, tender, chaste, untouched... Consciously or unconsciously, Lola continuously imbued me with these traits. Thus, as a young woman, my world rotated around the house, the church, the school and the marketplace. Anywhere else besides these places were "male territories" and a good girl like me had absolutely nothing to do there!

My unquestioning mind was also conditioned to value my purity or chastity to guarantee that I would reach the gates of heaven when I die. Yes, indeed I have not loved God as I ought to: I have feared Him so much. It drove me to refuse to venture into the "naughty world" of adolescents. I always refused classmates and friends whenever they invited me to parties, movies, lunch dates which would entail asking permission from my Lola. I excluded myself from any social and academic function and it was in such occasions that my religious scrupulosity became my "security blanket."

This myopic world view manifested itself in my schooling too. I went to school because it was the normal and ordinary thing to do. My early education and even my college education had not been significant enough to renew my consciousness as a woman. In fact my fear of academic failure pushed me to cling more and more to my novenas and devotion, my only means of deliverance from difficult situations.

Somehow, I managed to get by until I became a university faculty member in history and education. The academic world where I found myself was mostly composed of self made women-professionals, proto-types of contented beings who would even favor male dominance and manipulation just to climb the professional ladder. This set-up triggered my questioning self into action. The unanswered questions found their meaning when I started to compete in the realm of academic administration. I found the road to it quite thorny, rugged and most of all, lonely. It was really lonely up "there" that even a personal friendship with a man lost its meaning. I wonder now whether it was true love or just a ride on the common band wagon of having relationships. Further graduate studies augmented the degree of my professional growth but it also pointed to the fact that I have never matured emotionally as a person. I was still infantile in self-knowledge and understanding and that realization ran parallel to my image of God: the infant Jesus or Santo Niño, who was a God, and yet had not matured to complete independence and self-reliance.

In my late twenties, upon completing my doctoral program, I began to realize how far I have gone through life and wondered where else I would go... no where... and this scared me to the bones! Lola's demise and my parents' alienation made me scared and insecure. At this point of my life, I became fully aware that nobody could help me except myself.

I remember this period of aloneness as my opening to God. God whom I could call from my inner being, not because Lola and other people impelled me to do so! I felt I was hedged in and I longed for escape, but I could not... so I went deep down into my being and found that God was sleeping in my very essence. My aloneness disappeared and I started to face my ambivalent emotions... am I to marry someone following the ordinary course of a woman's life or pursue that haunting voice which kept on telling me that I could be in the school of the Lord's service, joining a missionary Benedictine congregation. The latter option prevailed as I faced the unacceptable reality that I have not really loved a man enough to be tied down by a marital commitment... only to find out that as a member of the religious sector, I have to love even more deeply and more sincerely!

The exact opposite of my personal expectations of what religious life was all about unraveled itself when I entered the convent as a postulant. Instead of keeping up my numerous devotions to saints and patrons of the church, my prayer life began to center alone on Jesus Christ, the God-Man. My change of name upon my novitiate initiation testified to this. Through my initial formation as a Missionary Benedictine novice and junior sister, God revealed Himself to me, not in doctrinal nor in theoretical studies, much less in unquestioning obedience, but in action, in working out a story of relationships.

My relationship with Christ found its expression in opportunities to take up the cause for truth, justice and freedom... being with striking workers to guard their picketlines against management intrusion and harassments; with the dead body of a certain Manny Lazo, shot during a peasants' rally in Liwasang Bonifacio simply because he stood for justice that must be upheld against the power that be; contending with military atrocities while on a fact-finding mission in Samar's massacres, strafing and hamletting of landless farmers with their helpless family members; overcoming fear to save a bleeding woman-fighter for justice and social transformation in Quezon Province and eventually giving her a decent burial to dramatize to everyone the dignity that God's children deserved. These stark realities, bigger than life, made me experience God in me and wherever people strive to be fully alive, the greatest springboard to love. These are events which make my vowed life as a Missionary Benedictine touch its core: God.

It is beautiful and very liberating to know that my God is alive... a God who is neither man or woman. He/She is everything, every event and every person I encounter as a religious woman. This also convinced me that God in Christ called me as His disciple to surrender in love to Him through service to His people. This surrender in love through service makes me drop all my defenses, my scruples, my facade. I allow the events and people in my life to reach gently into the secret element of my being to call forth a self I did not know was there!

Now that I am almost forty, I am fortunate as relationships grow in reciprocal vulnerability, allowing myself to be called forth by the other in an inclusive way, regardless of age, gender, social affiliation and beliefs.

Subsequently, my liberation as a woman started by revealing how good I felt by loving and being loved... If I am to grow and live, I must give and not just receive to bring about that fullness of life.

I must commit myself to this love, this Christ-life in others by sharing my presence in the now... ✿

Lourdes San Agustin

I grew up in a family that was patriarchal -- my father was the dominant figure, my mother, as well as we, the children, were obedient, submissive and passive. My parents were Roman Catholics but both were non-practising. The only time my father went to church was during Christmas and this, too, he has given up in the past years. My mother, on the other hand, does not hear mass at all but she prays a lot and is a devotee to several novenas and saints. At an early age, my image of God was very vague. I was not a regular churchgoer because I had no one to take after.

At times my mother would tell me, do not do that, do not do this because Papa Jesus will get angry. So, at an early age, my notion of God was male, just like my father who should always be pleased and obeyed. At home we had a picture of the Blessed Virgin Mary. My mother told me that she was the mother of Jesus, that's all.

In high school, I started to attend mass regularly. It was not because I found meaning in it or because I felt it was an obligation. It was because every Monday, our assignment in Religion was to discuss the gospel and the homily.

While in College at the University of Santo Tomas, I joined the Pax Romana, a religious organization where I, as a member, taught religion once a week in a public elementary school. Again, I did not do this because I wanted to please God or anything. I did it because as a member of the organization, I would be exempted from taking the final examination in Theology. It was in college, though, that I had a clearer image of Mary. My friends brought me along to Baclaran on Wednesdays and St. Jude on Thursdays. Now I see Mary not only as the mother of Jesus but as a woman whom I could turn to when problems arise. In a way I looked on her as my mother since I was staying with my grandmother.

As a young woman, my life revolved around the house, school and church. I soon realized that my grandmother, with whom I stayed while in college, was more strict than my father. I was practically not allowed to attend parties. Telephone calls were limited to five minutes, no dates. I excluded myself from social functions because I knew that I would not be allowed to go, so why bother to ask permission. Deep inside me I could not fully understand why. I was angry. I wanted to stand up and demand the reasons for such restrictions but our patriarchal set up crept in and told me: No, you should not question or go against the wishes of your elders because it is not proper, especially for a woman. I must say at this point religion oppressed me. It made me suppress all my anger, my disappointment and frustrations; obedience, submissiveness and passivity were strongly stressed.

In my early twenties, I could no longer take the restrictions at home and the seething anger in me gave way. I eloped and got married. The first five years of my marriage were almost perfect but somewhere along the way something went wrong. My husband and I decided to separate.

This crisis has changed my life. Before, I practically turned away from Christianity. It seemed to be a religion only of words. There was so much said on Sundays, but nothing seemed to come of it the rest of the week. The mass was meaningless to me and I thought I did not need God. All these changed when crisis struck. I did not turn my back on God. On the contrary, I felt that I had abandoned God for too long and I felt that I owe God so much.

I started to find meaning in prayers. In fact I learned how to compose my own prayers. I started to read the Bible and now I believe I have the Holy Spirit with me because my personal relationship with God produced love, joy, peace, patience, goodness, faithfulness, kindness, humility and self-control. With the help of my parents, relatives and friends, I soon recovered from my trauma. It was a painful experience but it definitely made me a stronger person, a better and more self-reliant human being.

Another crisis came to my life. Some of my co-teachers found out that I was separated from my husband. They made a big issue out of it. They reported to the administration that I was not fulfilling my non-academic requirements. There was even talk going around that I had a boyfriend. I felt so bad, I thought they were my friends. With my renewed faith in God, I was able to handle it. I can proudly say that I am ready emotionally, socially and spiritually for anything. I have my job and my children and I could not afford to wallow in self-pity. Life simply has to go on. I have learned to appreciate my own capacity to survive and manage stress. Now I can do things on my own. I feel a greater sense of competence and confidence. I also have my womenfriends to thank. They have accepted me and were willing to understand. In their company, I have known what sisterhood is all about.

Since my children and I made God a part of our lives, I feel we are continuously blessed. ஐ

Ka Odeng

I am a peasant woman. I was born to a poor family, the seventh among thirteen children.

We were a religious family. Every Sunday, my mother would take us, all 13 children, to the church to pray that God may give us His grace. In spite of our faithfulness, we continued to be poor and we continued to suffer.

In my mind, the question echoed and re-echoed: why are we still poor? My grandparents kept telling my parents, especially my mother, that we were poor because we still did not pray enough. The contradiction is that we have been praying, we have not done anything evil or wrong, yet nothing has changed. We were impoverished as ever.

My father was a peasant farmer by day. At night, he went fishing. In the morning, before going to school, if my father caught some fish, I would have to sell them. If he caught some frogs, those, too, I had to sell. I no longer aspired to go through high school because I wanted to help my parents earn a living.

If my parents were working in the field, I had to stay home, wash the clothes, do the cooking and take care of the rest of my sisters and brothers. I had to bring cooked meals to my parents at noon, help in the planting, and also in removing the weeds in the field.

As I grew up, the persistent questions in my mind were these: Why is it that even if my whole family was working on the land to the utmost, in spite of our sweat and labor, our conditions did not improve?

So I searched and asked: Why is the life of the peasant,

like this? What are its root causes? What are the reasons for our continuing poverty? When I heard that there were some studies going on regarding land reform, I decided to join the people who wanted to understand these problems.

When my mother heard that I was attending these study groups, she was angry and at times she would whip me and tell me, "You won't get anything out of these studies. It won't improve our lot as poor people." But slowly from these studies I started to understand our situation. So I had to explain to my parents that these studies symbolized the beginning of our long journey towards our people's betterment.

At 15 or 16, I began to understand the situation of the peasants in my village and throughout the rest of the country. I started to conduct some discussions among the women and young people in our village.

At 17, I got married. I have five children. My husband and I had been organizers in our village. We conducted educational programs among the villagers.

My husband was killed by the military more than a year ago. His death came as a shock to me. The military treated him like a pig. They told him that he was too smart so they hacked his head. His face was sliced on both cheeks, his mouth was used as an ashtray, his hands were pounded into a pulp. His arm was cut off because the military said he had been trying to teach the village folk. His legs were broken and then cut off because they said he had been going around the whole province, teaching his fellow peasants to become strong before their oppressors.

He pleaded for his life and said, "Don't kill me, think of my family." In spite of that, they killed him.

Now, in spite of what the military had done, I have committed myself to the cause of our people. I told them that we have to continue our struggle because the plight of the peasantry has not changed, even under the new government. Surely God will be with us for he always takes the side of those who are oppressed.

As a woman, I pursue my task of organizing other peasant women, inspiring them to play significant roles in society and to gain dignity and identity.

I am convinced that as long as our rights are not respected and justice is not obtained, the peasant women in the Philippines will continue to struggle. We may lack resources but we have our commitment. I have learned in my life that it is not enough to pray. One has to do something if only to become free. ⊗

(translated from the Pampango)

Sr. Jannie

I belong to one of the tribes of the Cordillera – the Ifugaos. We are usually portrayed in the lowlands as pagans, head hunters, *ignorante*, uncivilized, with tails, etc. The people in the lowlands call themselves Christians. "Urgent!" they say, "The Ifugaos need to be 'christianized'." *Kunu!*

The baptismal certificate I acquired before entering the convent testifies that I was baptized a few days after I was born. I was given a saintly European name by an ICM Belgian missionary. My brothers and sisters were also given Christian names. My parents' names were more Spanish. My mother lived up to her name. She was a consolation to her family and was contemplative by heart. She was my first teacher in prayer not through giving me lectures but through her fidelity to her early morning prayers (now I can call it meditation).

We were made to understand that Christian names were more acceptable, superior and more pleasant to the ears. Those who had native names were laughed at and discriminated. (At the gate of heaven, St. Peter might not accept souls with strange-sounding native names.) I had to pray the rosary doubly hard and I offered a lot of sacrifices for the repose of the souls of my ancestors who died without baptism, without Christian names. My catechetics teacher said that my ancestors' souls will be purified in purgatory. Another name for purgatory is "limbo" – a dark, cold and lonely place where the pained wailing of unbaptized babies and the agonized crying of pagan adults can be heard. With these concepts, I developed fear of the dark and fear of death.

Catechetics was considered number one subject in our Parish School. In my experience, it was always the first subject in the morning and number one in the grading sheet. And the pupil who was the highest pointer in this subject was awarded a special honor at the end of the schoolyear: "First in Religion!"

I learned to love this subject because of the colorful visual aids of Biblical themes that lined our classroom walls. Pictures of Abraham and Isaac, Moses, Jacob, the Israelites passing through the Red Sea (my favorite), Baby Jesus in the manger, Jesus at the Last Supper, the Blessed Virgin Mary in her blue gown and gold crown are still vivid in my memory until today. There were also pictures that haunted me as a child. Our teacher used to threaten or scold us with those pictures when we were noisy, irritated, tardy, when we fought with other children, when we disobeyed and forgot to say our prayers. Here is something I can draw from memory:

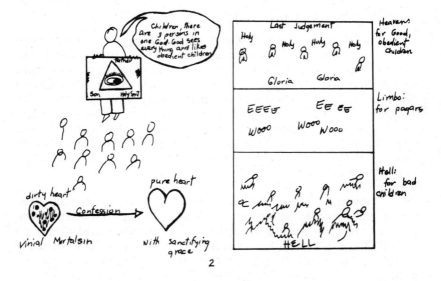

Such lessons were very successful in mystifying and domesticating the animist within us. This spirit was eventually alienated from my tribal nature. I became passive and sometimes confused. Soon, I lost my capacity to rely on collective efforts to face the daily problems that confronted us as children. I became an individualist and developed a moralistic attitude. At an early age, the "police force" within me began to work: charging myself guilty when I missed the early morning mass because I overslept; guilty because I followed other kids in climbing trees and eating too much guavas without permission; guilty because I joined the boys of my age group and dared to go mountain-climbing and swimming against the current of the roaring river. Yes, I found myself guilty but quietly admirable for courageously facing the consequences -- I received beatings from the belt of my very angry father (who said that as a little girl I should not do such things). I was also branded as a "tomboy" by our neighbors. I cried my heart out after that experience not only because of the painful beatings and the discrimination but more so because I discovered something about myself: I can dare! I can risk!

More and more, the effect of the religious instructions were reinforced by other academic concepts and activities. Positive and negative concepts were hammered into my simple mind. The soft brain in my head absorbed them all. Even as a young woman, the "police force" within me was very active. It made me very scrupulous and narrow-minded. It prevented me from building friendships and relating genuinely with other peers in the dormitory and at school because they belonged to other sectarian religions. The moralistic attitude within me negated my boyfriend's and my own expression of affection. When I gave in to a kiss or a hug, I had to suffer an aftermath — guilty conscience... sin against purity! I sensed something was wrong. But my simple mind then did not understand why.

I realize now that I had a "split spirituality": the "Christian" in me claimed to be superior, right and dogmatic. But deep down in my gut, the tribal spirit was telling me that there was something wrong, something alien. Within me, that spirit was rebelling. I, then, did not understand why. There was a contradiction within me but I learned to live with it through the years. The positive effect of that contradiction kept me open, alert and spurred me to explore... to move on... to search for unity.

The moralistic attitude and scrupulous minds were also true of other Christians like me. I personally experienced being judged, discriminated, prejudiced and even being labeled "communist" because of my background, and the latest, because of my belief in Jesus Christ who continually calls us to incarnate our Christianity, to give it flesh and blood in our service to God's *anawim* today.

Of late, I had such an experience as I had my homeleave last summer. My mother (a daily massgoer) naturally asked me how I was, my sisters in the convent, and the apostolate among the Negritos. I enthusiastically shared my stories! After a while, she took a deep breath, looked straight into my eyes and asked me, "Are you a communist?" My initial feeling was one of pain—pain of being judged, of being branded by a person I love so much. After a long tearful dialogue, the pain eased. My mother asked the question out of sincere concern for her daughter. My mother (being a victim of the red scare) cannot fit in the religious option I chose and the activities I am involved in into her traditional concept of a nun. I do not expect my mother to understand me immediately. I understand that it will be a painful process before she can or will accept the emerging image of a nun in her daughter. But I will be with her and wait for her patiently. In time, she will understand and be liberated from her confining views.

These experiences I call "limbo" experiences! According to my religion teacher of long ago, the "limbo" is a place of purification. In the light of my experiences, I see it now as a *state* of purification, of testing one's motives, one's faith, one's spirituality. After the limbo state is the "heaven state of liberation."

I could still recall that moment when I finally made the major decision to become a missionary. That feeling of triumph and liberation was so strong. Peace overwhelmed me. I cried over that feeling with sheer joy! That feeling came back again and again—many times, in many ways, in different places. Until now, inspiring, empowering!

In the convent, we, religious in formation, are taught to experience the Biblical texts in the light of the social, political and cultural situation of our country and the world. For me, this process is something new yet so familiar. This time, the God I read and experience in the Bible is different from the God I knew from my childhood. He was no longer a threatening God. He became the liberating God of the Israelites who dared to cross the Red Sea. He is familiar to me. This is the same God who challenged Abraham and Moses and now, me. He became the God who kept calling.

It was not easy to respond. Like Jacob, I had to grapple with Him. He challenged me to expose myself to the critical situation of our country. It was sometimes difficult and confusing. Amid this confusion, I met the simple Jewish girl, Mary. She was no longer the Mary with the long blue gown and golden crown. Slowly and gently, she removed the blind-fold from my eyes and made me see the sufferings of my people from her point of view—from my people's point of view. Her question of "How can this be?" became my own question. I followed her to the "hill country"... to the farmers, to the picketlines of the factory workers, to the fishermen's boats, to the huts and *kaingins* of the Negritos and the Mangyans... into the very heart of the problems, struggles and aspirations of all those people. Their struggle became my own.

My friends and I slept and ate with them. We discussed and studied together. We grappled with the different problems and analyzed situations prayerfully. A new consciousness was born! We had a reason to celebrate together. Within me, something was taking place... a change of perception about the situation, about myself, my understanding of Mary, her son's mission and the proclamation of the Gospel. Is that not liberation?

Yes, that is liberation. It is just like coming home. It is coming home to my people. It is coming home to myself. It is coming home to God.

It was also liberation when I realized that the religion I hold and cherish had to pass through "limbo" to be tested and to be renewed.

It was liberation when I continued to allow myself to be challenged by Faith and religion to respond and join other people—people of integrity and commitment, people who love freedom. They are the peasants, the workers, the tribal Filipinos, students, the women and church people, ready to lay down their lives for their friends.

It was liberation when I allowed religion to help me root out the cause of our basic problems, and be fearless to face the powerful enemies that assault, dominate and eliminate us physically and culturally. Through faith, I was able to see clearly and be alerted by the enemy's purpose to usurp and control our homeland, natural bounties and even our women.

It was liberation to experience the inspiring effect of faith-experiences and reflections that resonate with the tribal spirit within me. Also, getting to know the person of Mary of the Magnificat has taught me to incarnate the Christian faith within me.

I affirm that religion has liberated me (is still liberating me) for it has set forth and empowered that spirit which urges me to unite with people of other Faiths—Muslims, Protestants, Hindus and yes, even the atheists—in order to overcome division and to be one with our people and their struggle to hasten total liberation! 🞝

Sr. Ester

It is late in the evening and I sit here on my bed beside my window with the mosquitos as my ever-loyal companion, and I ask myself, why am I having a difficult time starting this paper on my life and how religion oppressed and liberated me? In the three other occasions I started to write but did not continue, I caught myself praying to the Holy Spirit to liberate me from the block that I felt was keeping me from getting a head start. I pray to the Holy Spirit when I experience similar blocks... and most of the time I do get "liberated" from the initial chaos of my mind. Sounds childish doesn't it... having to rely on a divine force to get anything done? Upon deeper reflection I get to see that it is at these moments of prayer that I calm myself, concentrate on the task at hand and get my thoughts organized. During these instances I come up with an "enlightened" energy. The Holy Spirit incarnated!

This is the way I approach my faith—a God in context. A God who works in people, in experiences, and in history... devoid of all the magical trappings that a lot of Catholics still hang on to. I have developed this spirituality only when I entered the convent. I have only really *lived* when I started to form this type of spirituality during the early years of my Novitiate. There were so many people and events that led to this... but before I do relate them I would like to recall my past and the reasons why I found it difficult to get a head start on this paper.

Most of my early religious experiences were not very formative in the sense that I did not become very religious when I grew up. I find it difficult to pinpoint experiences that led me to feel liberated or oppressed by my religion because I was not entirely conscious of my religion then.

My family was not the *Katoliko-sarado-nakakandado*

type. We followed Roman Catholic rules and regulations to the minimum like regularly attending Sunday Mass, confession at least once a year (before Christmas), not killing anybody, not commiting adultery (or if anyone in the family did so, I never got to know about it), and to put a seal on all these, we, the children, went to study in a Catholic school run by Religious Sisters. My family was considered as one of the "well brought up" families in the small city where we lived. We did not see any need to demand more from ourselves in terms of being religious. This Catholic upbringing I count as a blessing because I had no hardened religious beliefs that need to be undone - not even the usual Catholic devotions like the rosaries, novenas, etc., not that these devotions need to be "undone" but I never had any hang up about them.

With this foreword on my past, let me now concretely relate my religious experiences.

"Forgive me, Father for I have sinned," went little Ester as she knelt before her regular Grade School Confessor with the usual screen window between them, "it has been one week since my last confession. These are my sins:

> *I fought with my brother.*
> *I backbited my sister.*
> *And I said bad words.*
> *I am sorry for them."*

After sighing with relief for having gone over the worst of rituals, little Sonia waited for her penance which was the usual one Hail Mary, one Our Father and one Glory Be. To her surprise, the priest broke the tradition and asked her, "Do you regularly go to Sunday Mass?"

"Yes, Father."
"Do you love and obey our parents?"
"Yes, Father."

By this time, little Sonia was wondering why the priest wanted to add more to her sins. However, he continued, "Well child, your sins are not really big ones. They are just little venial sins. You can go now. I don't have to give you any penance for them."

I remember leaving the Confessional feeling quite elated

for not having committed big sins and quite liberated from going through the regular ritual of confession until I have committed a BIG sin.

I remember too, one of the few times I prayed the rosary when I was a child. With not much understanding of its value, my cousins and I complied with my Lola's urgings to kneel as we prayed the rosary before her altar of the Sacred Heart of Jesus where a wooden rosary was used as a backdrop. By the time we reached the long litany of the Blessed Virgin Mary, we, the younger ones... were already seated on our heels and were giggling as we responded, "Pray for rice" to every litany... little did I know then that we were quite correct in making such a contextualized response.

If my Lola was a very devout Catholic who went to mass everyday and had a devotion to our Lady of Mt. Carmel (thus, her eternal brown attire), my Lolo, on the other hand, was one who did not blink an eyelash out of guilt for questioning the Bible. He was an educated man, a lawyer-accountant who has read the Torah, the Koran, the Bible and others.

I remember little Sonia listening to her Lolo with her chin on her hands as he asked, "Why do Catholics call Mary the Mother of God when Jesus never called himself God but 'Son of Man'?" Of course her Lolo never expected her to answer his questions but for Ester that experience of guiltless questioning also found a home in her heart.

Some unpleasant "religious" experiences that come to mind right now do not exactly deal with religion directly oppressing me but they deal with a feeling of oppression and discrimination coming from the preaching of those considered "Religious". I studied in an exclusive Catholic Girl's School run by Religious Sisters. During my Grade School days, I was one of the students who did not figure prominently economically, intellectually, physically, or what have you... and I was indirectly made to feel my insignificance by the way the Sisters related to me and my kind and the way I, too, related to them.

Little Ester does not really understand the term discrimination or prejudice but it did leave its mark on her. For instance there was this time when Ester confused the meaning of the term "prostitute" to mean "prejudice". So, one afternoon, coming home from school after having been discriminated by one of the Sisters, Ester went straight to her Nanay to report indignantly. "Alam mo, 'Nay, si Sister-teacher namin ay 'prostitute' sa akin." ("You know, Ma, our sister-teacher 'prostituted' me.") Her mother and her sister, who was also present, looked at each other to figure out what Ester was trying to say.

The discrimination was felt even more when one day it was announced that the whole class would go to watch a movie in a down-town theater and *everyone* was to take public transportation to get there... well, that is, everyone except our Sister-teacher and our classmate who rode on our classmate-owned Mercedes Benz. Later, we learned that the night before, the Sister called our classmate to ask if she could kindly bring the family car for the next day's activity.

Ester, by the time she hit third year College experienced her first big crisis - a crisis of identify. She knew there was more to life then what she was doing then - trying to finish a degree. She felt her life was going down the drain. Of course she consulted a lot of people about her situation but none of their answers nor pieces of advice seemed to fit... The school's guidance counselor needed to be listened to more than she did; the priest she went to always offered high falluting theological solutions, her friends were just in the same boat as she, her parents, she presumed would not understand.

Two years this crisis lasted. Two years of just existing, doing the usual routine of studying, having fun with friends, and staying at home with the family but still feeling the rut inside. One day, after these two long years, I found myself at the back seat of our School Chapel... not really praying those formula prayers we were taught in school but just sitting there. It felt good! Within me, there was a sense of "coming home," a sense of peace. There was no urgency to try to understand my situation, no pressure to be anything at all. I did not feel that I was being judged for being in a rut. I was just being ME—just ME before my Lord! I didn't ask anything from him either (I considered Him as a male God then). So, after that day, like the parched ground that has tasted sweet water, I found myself at the Chapel almost everyday, just *being.* Once in a while I would attend daily masses or novenas but they didn't have any meaning for me then. I didn't want to try so hard to find the meaning of life in the rituals that didn't resound within me. There was, for a while, the tendency to project my needs on the Holy Eucharist and on the novenas but it did not last. It did not answer my new-found need to just *be.*

I believe my experiences—the confession, the contex-tualized rosary, the guiltless questioning and being discrimi-nated—all formed the basic desire within me to find meaning in life. Here started my *conversion* to faith—the blossoming of a dormant spirituality that breathed with passion for life. This started when I came upon an insight that changed my life. One year after graduation, I entered the convent.

Change my life? It most certainly did and what more, it liberated me and now I am really *alive.* I learned that to question was not wrong—not even if it is the Bible I put in question... my Lolo was right after all. I got answers that further enlightened me about my faith but I certainly did not lose my love for the Bible. However, with the answers came more questions, only for me to discover that I have been what is often called a "Christian in name only." The Lord certainly worked on my passionate nature, because once I knew this, I set my heart in following the path of making my life meaning-ful.

One of the beautiful structures in my Novitiate life was making the poor part of my life. This entailed difficult adjust-ments that mainly have to do with journeying from a ME-perspective to an US-perspective. It was difficult because it demanded that I transcend, not suppress, my need for greater value. For example one of the basic objections to going for an area apostolate to the nearby slum areas on a Saturday after-noon was that it shortened my siesta time. Sleep was important for me specially after having tired myself out with work for a whole week. But letting the people into my life made me realize that I could make do with a 45-minute siesta instead of an hour and a half. This awakening sense of solida-rity with the poor was brought to a greater understanding of the perspective of the poor when I went for my first 5-day im-mersion program. The following is a post-reflection I made on my experience with the fishermen and women in the light of understanding my vow of poverty.

There is a lot of truth in the statement, "We religious, make the vow of poverty but it is the people who live it." My Dialogue of Life with the poor fishermen was a clear experience of poverty – not only of my poverty but more so, the people's poverty.

The people's poverty can be based on three models of poverty, namely, *poverty as communitarian sharing:* Poor as they are, the fishermen still shared with their fellow fishermen their material goods like food. When a fisherman knows that his friend had a meager catch, he would share his supper little though it may be. When I arrived at my foster cousin's place, it was at a time when the motor of his banca was out of order. So his neighbor shared the use of his banca with him so that, through their collective efforts, both their families would have something to eat for the day. Another fisherman friend of theirs would come some afternoon to try to fix the motor without charge and one day, the motor started!

The people felt for each other and cared for each other They were united in heart and mind.

Poverty as simplicity of life: This I saw, was very much lived to the full by the community leaders like Kuya Andy and Kuya Tanio. They share their time, talent, person, etc. with their people and also with people like us in order that they may attain for themselves and for their fellow Filipinos a life that is built on justice, peace and love.

For me the model of poverty which I experienced there was *poverty as union with the poor and oppressed:* My immersion with them made me experience the hunger they experience, the joy of sharing meals with the neighbor, the shared anticipation of waiting whether the motor would get fixed or not, the late coffee-filled nights joining their *pulong* (meetings) and so many more. However, further reflection revealed me to deeper union with them which lay in this model of poverty. The late nights shared with them in *pulong* were the most delicate time of my stay there. One night, while we were in the middle of the meeting, we heard a man knock on the wall of the house, a signal which meant that there was an outsider approaching. Kuya Andy immediately signalled me to leave the room and hide myself behind a cupboard, as previously arranged. My fear was clearly manifested in the way the front of my blouse would move in rhythm with the beating of my heart.

There was also an instance when I had to walk a distance at night with two men in order to attend a meeting in another house. I had to dress and walk as a man and put a towel over my head to disguise myself. The walk, going to and coming from the house, was filled with anticipation. I would look for places where I could run to just in case we were found out. In this sense, I also shared with them their fear of being caught.

Our class in Ecclesiology gave us a beautiful point for reflection. The Roman Church as it is, is built on an hierarchical structure with Peter, the rock—the foundation of the Church, as the basis for such a structure. However, contemporary theology challenges such a structure of the Church—a structure which has reproduced the authority of Peter in the person of the Pope, Bishops, etc.—because, through the Church's many doctrines and guidelines, the faithful has been led to a complacent way of living. As long as one follows the Law and obeys it, one is saved.

Reading the Bible once more and contextualizing it in our present situation, a new insight will be gained, that is, our response to the call of salvation by God, through Christ, is made through *discipleship* -- to follow Christ in his involvement, to get out of our too familiar surroundings and create a contradiction to a complacent society.

I made this paper on Poverty almost 6 years ago. From then on, with my gradual involvement in other people's lives I also got more and more involved with the Bible and its message. The Bible came alive!... and still more alive when I went to study Theology, Sociology, Psychology in an Institute which was also committed to a thrust of Solidarity with the Poor... and still more alive when I got more deeply involved in people's mass actions and organizations where they showed me that the Word of God is *liberating!*... and still becoming more alive now that I know our God is beyond all the images we were taught in school and even beyond gender.

With the Bible and my experiences with the people bringing me to a full life, I now realize how oppressive our religion is indeed. I was precisely a Christian in name only because my religion did not demand more from me when it should have. My religion has limited faith to a personalized relationship with God instead of pursuing a communitarian perspective! My religion has stagnated its followers to a stage of mediocrity by not challenging them to go beyond just receiving the sacraments!

Right now as I write this, my whole being is crying out against such an oppressive religion. No wonder I did not find any meaning in life. For people who have a passion for life, they would need to go beyond all that would oppress them, even their religion, if they are to be true to the Lord's promise of a life lived to the *full*! 🞉

Pia Crisostomo Arboleda

For thirteen years, I studied in a school run by nuns. I guess that makes me 'convent-bred'. My mother, being deeply religious, did not settle for anything less than a good Catholic education for me. Today, five years after my high school graduation, I look back into my childhood with fondness though not without recalling the trauma.

When I was in prep school, aged six, I always had difficulty in asking permission whenever it was time to go to the bathroom. Sitting near the door did not help—the evil door tempted me to sneak out. Discovering this, my teacher got very upset. (She must have really missed me.) She scolded me and said, "kneel and say sorry to Jesus," whose image appeared above the blackboard. In front of the whole class I received my punishment. Since then, I regarded God as someone who punished disobedient little girls. (I always thought that only little boys had the right to be naughty.)

In grade school, my friends and I were introduced to a lot of religious rituals. Five times a day we prayed—first thing in the morning, before and after recess, before and after lunch, and at the end of the day. If we were 'lucky', we got to pray before and after each subject, too. This routine extended itself all the way to high school when we did it with a twist. We combed our hair, we copied assignments, we talked about our crushes, we did a lot of 'unholy' things while we prayed. Eventually, this form of prayer lost its meaning for me and I refused to pray.

Every first Friday of the month, we went to celebrate mass. At the chapel we sat, six girls to a pew. Our teachers made sure we did not sit too close to each other so we would avoid engaging in girlish chatter in the "sacred house of God." Still, some Fridays were more difficult than others because our best jokes were told at the chapel. Little grade school girls were at their wittiest while celebrating the Eucharist.

We went to confession once every schoolyear. At fourth grade, I was absent on the day our section went to confession. This caused me to dread my fifth grade confession for I knew that the priest would ask me when I last received this sacrament. At age ten, I was convinced that this ritual's main purpose was to give a person demerits (like in Citizen's Army Training) and to make us feel guilty for days on end.

Every October was Holy Rosary month, the time Virgin Mary's statue is passed around from classroom to classroom and we prayed a whole mystery. I was indifferent to this custom which mainly took the time off the lectures of my boring teachers. But most prominent among my rosary memories is my Tia Anunciacion (named after the first joyful mystery).

Vacationing in Bacolod one summer, I stayed in her villa. She would require my cousins and me to pray the rosary every night without fail or else we would be 'court marshalled.' I tried many tactics to get myself excused—walking the dog, feigning endless dysmenorrhea—but nothing worked. It was bad enough to kneel on wooden floors; it was even worse to find out that my male cousins were exempted. *Boys* were "naturally irreverent" anyway, but *girls* need to be religious and pious. Or so she said. What great disappointment it must be for her to know that I still cannot recite the Hail Holy Queen from memory. From what I can remember, there was something about it that needed re-visioning. So recently, I chose to rewrite it to present an alternative image of Mary and to dramatize the power available to all women.

It was also from Tia Ansyang that I discovered what my name meant. She said that I should be proud but when I found out that my name translates into 'pious', I almost puked. I was hardly *that!* Why couldn't they have baptized me with a name that meant 'beautiful' or 'dearest' or *any*thing besides 'pious'?! (At that time it was not yet my wish to be named after 'wisdom' or 'strength'.)

My family went to mass every Sunday. My parents always taught us that we will be blessed because we know how to pay respects to the Lord. But I only looked forward to it because we would go to the movies afterwards. This was to be the subject of family disagreements when my brother and I reached college and refused to go to Sunday mass. My parents feel that it is their responsibility to save our souls especially in the event that the much-heralded calamity of "three days of darkness" strikes. I was called a communist; my brother was said to have followed my footsteps by being very stubborn and disobedient. True to our labels, we didn't go any way.

In high school, when I first started to attend parties, I had to observe a curfew like most girls my age. My parents would get worried when I am not home by midnight. (They read Cinderella once too often.) Out of concern, they would scold me and later my father would show me a verse in the Bible (Sirach 42:9-14), the source of all my guilt feelings as a woman. It read:

> A daughter is a treasure
>> that keeps her father wakeful
>> and worry over her drives away rest:
> Lest she pass her prime unmarried,
>> or when she is married, lest she be disliked:
> While unmarried, lest she be seduced,
>> or, as a wife, lest she prove unfaithful,
> Lest she conceive in her father's home,
>> or be sterile in that of her husband.
> Keep a close watch on your daughter,
>> lest she make you the sport of your enemies,
> A byword in the city, a reproach among the people,
>> an object of derision in public gatherings.
> See that there is no lattice in her room,
>> no place that overlooks the approaches of the house.
> Let her not parade her charms before men,
>> or spend her time with married women;
> For just as moths come from garments,
>> so harm to women comes from women:
> Better a man's harshness than a woman's indulgence,
>> and a frightened daughter than any disgrace.

I never touched the Bible again because I felt that it can be abused to control my life!

For college, I was convinced that I needed a change of scenery so I went to a university only to be disturbed by the Angelus every noon and sundown. Like machines, we would turn off whatever we were doing and pray. Even in the middle of a tormenting Calculus test, the Angelus would taunt me.

The scenery did not change and my training was not all that relevant either. Sure, going to this school provided me with a prestigious name to put in my resume but it left no mark within me. What was most significant in my stay there, however, was my introduction to a deep social concern for my people and my country which, ironically, I did not develop inside the classrooms of this "Christian" university.

I found it instead in the ranks of the masses—first as a mere observer of the plight of the Smokey Mountain community, eventually as a participant in the peasants' *lakbayan* from Bulacan to Liwasang Bonifacio. I got involved in discussion groups, integration sessions, the *Welgang Bayan*, the wake and funeral marches for Lean and Ka Lando. I learned to survive without the arrogance and excesses of bourgeois living, making do with life's barest essentials.

The revolutionary Christ was introduced to me. A Christ who questioned the status quo and opposed the control of the Pharisees, whose miracles worked in the hearts and minds of the men and women who later became his apostles. He made the 'blind' see the oppression of the poor, the 'deaf' hear the good news of God's reign in a world of equality. The dead (those who fought for freedom) he raised, only to live forever in every *kasama* who believes in the concrete salvation of the people. He was a Christ who spoke to the woman at the well though it was forbidden, who believed in female discipleship, who spoke of "longing to gather (Jerusalem's) children, as the hen gathers her chicks under her wings."

Following the footsteps of such a Christ, my old school broadened this vision of nurturance, teaching me about God the Mother, the courageous women-leaders in the Bible, the new images of Eve, Magdalene and the Virgin Mary. Because of this vision, no one can use the Bible to make me feel guilty, no one can take my womanhood against me. This new perspective gives me a "a glimpse of the world through God's eyes,"* revealing that justice springs from equality.

Back in the school of my childhood, I feel I have come home. I realize now that it sowed the seeds of womanrevolution within me. It has grown as I have, mature in wisdom and strength. Daily, I see its seal with two inscriptions—prayer and work. One day soon, I hope, it will be able to add one more: freedom. ⊞

---

*Isak Denesen

Yasmin Flores

I grew up in Lucban and Tayabas (Quezon Province) where my maternal grandmother who raised me comes from. As the seventh child of my mother's nine children, my Lola asked my mother that I be "given" to her for caring and companionship in her old age. My mother being an only child understood her and so barely six months old I was brought to Quezon to live with my grandmother.

If genetics and childhood environment have anything to do with one's spirituality, then Lucban and Tayabas must have helped shape my early experience of God. I would say religion is something else. It would come to me as formal knowledge when I attended primary school in Lucena some years later. Anyway, in these quiet, nature-filled towns (we live in Tayabas but spend week-ends in Lucban), blue mountains, green trees, multicolored flowers, clean streams, fresh fruits and milk were everyday experience. Nature's beauty and abundance filled my young senses. I simply knew God exists and is good to people.

This great feeling of oneness with nature would grow whenever my uncle priest brought us (nephews and nieces) to picnics. Sometimes in the mountains, at times by the beach, more often in the family coconut plantation. Always with so much food and fun especially when my seminarian cousins went along. (At one time there were three of them in the seminary). They were such good company. Crazy and playful as the rest of us, I later wondered and could not believe they were the same cousins I played and joked with because they looked so solemn and holy in their ordination clothes some years hence.

I've often wondered why my maternal grandfather lived in a cozy little house outside the town and not with us. Later I was to know that my grandmother and he were separated by fact and not necessarily by law. I learned that it had to do with my grandmother's refusal to put up with his fondness for women and gambling, the latter vice which he pursued to death. Literally to death because he had a hypertension attack while in a mahjong session. I have not forgotten the memory of the day he died. He was finally brought home for the wake. My Lola dressed me up for the funeral in a beautiful pink dress with little green dots. I wondered why my dress was so festive while the others wore either black or white. Could my Lola have felt relieved, after all, and my dress subconsciously expressed it?

I seldom saw my parents. All I could remember were the summer months when they came for short visits. But that was all. It was kind of lonely seeing them off at the train station at the end of summers. Could this be the reason why up to my teen years I have always felt ambivalent about summer? But I had a happy childhood despite everything.

What has this to do with religion? Quite a lot, I would say. Early in life I developed this habit of talking to Someone up there for comfort and understanding in moments of sadness or joy, achievements or failures, life or death. Perhaps, I was left pretty much to myself as a child. Hence this early self-communication and building of an interior self. Lola was often busy in her bakery, grocery and coffee shop. She would also leave for days on end to visit and supervise the coconut plantation in Gumaca.

That was when I would find the company of an aunt (vacationing and recuperating from acute anemia) such a pleasant substitute. It was she, Tia Payang, who would spend hours telling me children's stories and legends famous in this or that province. She also introduced me to Bible stories. My favorites were San Isidro, the farmers' saint; San Fernando, the saint who was King; and Mary, the beautiful mother of God. She has a way of telling stories to children, as if they just happened yesterday. Funny but she did not distinguish between legends of Banahaw and Makiling and the stories of Christmas, Good Friday and Easter. These were all told and retold with much gusto and pathos as the case may be. Thus, to my young imaginative mind, people, fairies, saints, gods and goddesses criss-crossed this earth and the beyond like it was the most natural thing. In a way, magic and mysticism combined.

Being a lawyer she could at times be sharp or too frank with her views. So relatives often kidded me not to take after her for she was unlike most women "*may kapilosopohan, kaya hindi nakapag-asawa.*" Meaning she was too witty and argumentative she ended up unmarried. But I liked her for her open and direct way of dealing with people even with a child like me. It was from her that I learned to be honest. It is best to be truthful and to thine own self one must be true above all.

I went to school at age six. Rather late for my contemporaries. But Tia Payang was such a good mentor and friend. She had laid a good foundation in my education. When I went to Sacred Heart College in Lucena to study I really missed her. For months I could not eat or sleep well and would secretly cry in my room.

It was in the confines of a convent school that I first had my formal catechetical instruction. The nuns and the college chaplain taught us the rudiments of religion. But it was mostly rote learning and rather dull. Gone was the magic and drama of the Bible stories. It was worse for the legends, I never heard or read them at all. A lot of what was told and read consisted of how sinful mankind was and how devils roam the earth for victims like us. So much guilt and fear were being inculcated into our young minds, deliberately or not. But I was somehow resistant. I stuck to Tia Payang's version of legends and Bible stories, my fun-loving uncle priest and cousin seminarians' image of God as powerful but loving, just but forgiving (so long as we repent and rectify), not a God who was always threatening and punishing.

Lucena being a fast-growing town was then losing much of its rural character. So for a while, gone were the picnics in the mountainsides and firefly-hunting at night in the backyards or the parks. I also missed the rolling farmscapes where the cows, horses, chickens mingled with people in work and play. I saw how animals copulate and later actually deliver their young. The case of the birds and bees was easy to accept later on, also human reproduction when I reached high school.

But the opposite was happening in my elementary classes. No mention was made of how babies are born especially in religion. Sex was taboo and parts of the human body remained nameless. I remember how I had to confess my curiosity about how grown-ups make love and produce babies. I bought myself some forbidden magazines and comics and started imagining having sex myself. I was barely twelve then. And the priest had me pray the whole rosary as penance. How was it that love and the joy of expressing it seemed so wrong and evil, I asked myself then, a question which remained unspoken for many more years to come.

High school meant moving to Manila. I was sent to study at Holy Ghost College now College of the Holy Spirit, a school for girls run by German nuns. Though strict and rigorous with our studies, we had a balanced curriculum and extra-curricular activities. Besides our books, we had sports, the debating club, a choral group, the writers' pool, catechists cells; hospital visitation groups, outings and trips to botanical gardens, Balara filters, Tagaytay ridge, parties with San Beda and Ateneo boys.

Religion was also more fun now specially the Holy Retreats conducted by the Irish Columban priests or Jesuits. They were not only good-looking but were also open-minded enough to entertain childish and naughty questions from teeners like us. They were probably amused (though they did not show it) by our confessions of secret crushes on them! High school years seemed peaceful and happy as a whole.

To a teenager fresh from convent school, studying for college in UP was certainly exciting and challenging. For me the green and spacious Diliman campus was an added bonus. It revived the ambience of Lucban and Tayabas in some ways, especially in Decembers when it was cold and foggy.

This was in the mid-60s nearing the First Quarter Storm when the nationalist movement reached its peak in campuses, factories, farms, slums and other depressed areas of Philippine society. As a music student and later also a history major, I was torn between two opposite forces. The arts were apolitical pursuits then, while history was exposing me to the most radical ideas of the period from liberal demo-cracy to Marxism and Maoism. Reactionary and militant stu-dent organizations competed for our membership in this or that group. I joined the nationalist and militant ones (Bertrand Russell, SCAUP, UP Political Science Club) and later Movement for Advanced Nationalism or MAN. Earlier, I was an active member of the UP Student Catholic Action but I lost interest because it remained distant from all the ferment and important issues of the day and of society. It remained a religious association.

This was the time when my boyfriend and I began to quarrel over which should come first, studies or rallies, politics or art. Theoretically, he always won the argument. Music was a demanding course that required at least five hours of practice at the piano. But I told him my dream of becoming a pianist was beginning to fade in the face of so much change taking place in practically all spheres of society and we were so indifferent to it all. Strange that he could not understand my restlessness and desire to participate in helping other people specially the poor among us who fight for the most basic things such as food, shelter, education when we both had so much including freedom.

Later, I went to vigils, pickets and demonstrations with people I hardly knew. It irritated him that I would spend hours listening to DGs (discussion groups of activist professors and students) and find no time to attend choir rehearsals and concerts with him, or that I dropped out from UPSCA because retreats, catechetical teachings and charity work were beginning to lose their appeal. By then I had started to queston the faith that declares itself for the poor but would not stand by the oppressed when being bashed by truncheons and tear-gas or when put to jail. Church people then feared Reds in the abstract and refused to see people in the concrete —dying that others may live decently.

By then, too, I read practically all books with nationalist content: Recto, Constantino, Joema Sison, Tanada, Diokno, Marx, Lenin, Mao, Ho Chi Minh. I listened to fiery speeches in Plaza Miranda, before the Congress, Liwasang Bonifacio, Mendiola, Plaza Moriones and Balintawak, not knowing that this was to be the beginning of a life-time commitment: to free the country and restructure society. Who could predict then that the young people who braved the police and military assaults would in the future face bigger storms? I will never forget how students and workers were brutally attacked in front of Congress in that infamous January opening of the parliament. Bullets literally flew above our heads as we docked behind the walls.

I was a young history professor at the University of the East when Martial Law was declared. As one of the teachers active in the faculty strike and in campus teach-ins, the university administration saw an opportune excuse to dismiss nine of us under PD 1081. Under this notorious decree all faculty members and students even without proof but suspected to be activists were to be expelled as "subversives." It was a shocking experience to us despite a foretaste of things to come (earlier was the suspension of the Writ which sent some of our friends, colleagues and students to the underground) and intelligent predictions of martial rule.

The early years of Martial Law were harrowing ones. One would rather forget them. Jobless and fearful for our lives most activists sought the help of families and sympathetic friends for survival and sanity. Religion was farthest from my mind having been taught by historical materialism to rely on our own strength and struggles. With so much violence being heaped against the people and with the church so silent about it, I saw no reason why prayers and going to mass would be of any help to the hunted. It was a dark period for me spiritually. I was hurt and angry why God was so silent through it all. I stopped going to church except out of necessity to attend the funerals of dead comrades and friends.

Of course, I was not blaming God. I just could not relate activism and people's struggle with my childhood faith. Succeeding events would lead to some answers. Blacklisted from teaching I ended up as a researcher for individual scholars and later for private and government agencies. The shift in my job was a blessing in disguise. I developed new skills and interests, met new friends and considered new forms of commitment. At this point a major change in my life took place. I began to consider a new form of activism in a new terrain—research and analysis for the people.

By 1980 I was working part-time with a church group engaged in people-oriented research. For the first time I found the answer to that aching gap inside--the dichotomy between religion and politics. I became part of church people engaged in liberation of both body and soul, religious and lay people who risked their lives for the poor, deprived, and oppressed. Gone was a life of isolation in the convents, endless prayers and charity work. Together we participated in the small people's struggles wherever it took us. I will never forget the brutal death of a fellow church worker in the hands of supposedly "drug addicts" out to rob him. Thirty stab wounds at a young age of thirty-two. His only crime was teaching the workers how to write their own manifestos and research into their working conditions. Others like him were to follow the same terrible end, death by salvaging as it is called. Or death-squad killings as part of counter-insurgency programs.

I no longer doubt that God is with us in this struggle of national liberation. God is in history and in every death and victory of the worker, the peasant, the urban poor; in the sacrifices of the conscienticized middle class and foreign solidarity friends. That gap has been bridged but what about religion, politics and my personal life, my love and marriage intertwined with our vision for a just and humane society? Few people would understand why I would persist in a "marriage" or relationship that has been declared by law to be null and void from the start. But God knows that it is not so much the persistence to keep a form intact but a belief in freeing love relationships from the stifling conventions and laws so that marriages and families may be truly honest and free.

There are times I feel crushed. Oh God, I often pray, how can this struggle be ended so we can find peace and freedom? Not through our laws which are outdated and not through our courts which prefer the letter to the spirit of the law. Not through the movement either. Would cause-oriented groups take up annulment and divorce as equally important issues as land reform, military bases, vigilantes, poverty, prostitution, etcetera? That would be petty bourgeois and divisive. It would also create a backlash from the country's dominantly Catholic population.

Feminism provides the answer—this vision of a wholly free society. My feminist friends (lay and nuns) have been very supportive of my personal struggle to bridge this gap between religion, politics and personal love. Together we read and study, organize and struggle for new power relations and structures, new definitions and identities, for new beliefs and faiths. It is a difficult one because it encompasses the whole of life as lived. The whole of society in all its spheres: the economic, the political, the cultural, the sexual and spiritual.

Standing on a mountain side up North last year, my activist and artist friends and I found ourselves in communion with the immense and beautiful nature that is Sagada. For some moments we felt peace descend upon us as if some unknown energy or spirit has enveloped and energized us. And when the first star appeared in the horizon we felt no space, no emptiness, no gap between us and the whole cosmos. I was back in the fold of my childhood experience of God and religion. I was happy and sad at the same time. But not hopeless or defeated anymore. ෴

Eco

Religion played a big part in my life. It still does today. However, I would like to think that I have broadened my horizons and understanding of religion such that the person I am today has come through a process involving struggle, challenge and questioning. I do not think I have found all the answers (how dull if it were so!) but I have found peace in my soul and the courage of my convictions. Perhaps, this comes with age. Perhaps I have had time to ponder on truths and kernels of wisdom and now I am reaping its harvest.

I thought of the words "oppressed" and "liberated" as categories to judge the effect religion had in my life. Both oppression and liberation have occured at different stages in my life. As a child, until my 15th year, I did have an attraction to the study and practice of religion to what I would like to call my "captured years". I was attracted to priests and nuns because they seemed to be so important, so helpful, so vital and vibrant. I did not like their stories about hell but they seemed to know everything. I never liked rituals—going to mass, novenas, rosaries—that were so much a part of a Catholic's life, including abstinence and fasting. But I enjoyed listening to arguments about religion and philosophy, the ins and outs, how and why. The church institution seemed hollow with so much emphasis placed on empty rituals and their importance.

There is one aspect of me that has always been prominent—I questioned the basis of structures, their reasons for being and their subsequent practices. But it was hard to question at that tender age because no one explained anything and what more, you could be branded as a heretic! It was not an age of inquiry. Faith had to suffice.

When I was at second year high school. I joined the sodality. My moderator used innovative methods for meditation and listened to our questions. I was drawn to being a Catholic. Going through my adolescence, I suppose I felt an intensity and passion about life and how I could process it. Religion was only one way.

As I turned 14, my father died. His death crushed my world. I loved him very much and it seemed like the world was filled with darkness. Cynicism began to creep in; this abetted my natural rebelliousness. I began to question the very foundation of my faith and continued to do so until my 17th year. I was caught between questioning the death of a loved one and the logic of faith in an institutional church. A fusion came about and I was not happy with the arrangement. Religion became too personal, too blinded by hurt feelings. Still it was not easy to turn one's back on a religion you have practiced since childhood. I could not find anything to replace it. I questioned. Sometimes, I felt God in me, peace within me. More often, I was rebelling and resisting but I could not seem to pinpoint exactly what it was I rebelled against. I just knew I could not accept the way the Church handed down doctrine—what was faith, the honesty and authenticity of my personal values and beliefs, where God came in, if God did exist.

I soon met the man who would be my husband. Our relationship touched on the role of God in us. Being both Catholics willing to live the faith, we had to thresh things out. We held long discussions on religion and philosophy. He knew (still does) so much more than I did but best of all, his faith was, as it is today, solid as a rock. Finding answers and initiating dialogue with other friends and groups was, for me, a way back to the Church. I had realized then that the Church had opened its doors, having come up with Vatican II.

As I grew older, I still had many questions, my rebelliousness. The structure of the Church and its institutionalized hierarchy and worship turned me off all the more. I plunged into my period of intense reading on anything under the sun, and as I read more, I questioned more.

I turned more and more secular but I did not feel heretical; a bit atheistic, if there is such a thing. I was liberating myself from religion "on one's sleeves" but yet I was doing more for my fellowmen. More and more the concepts of social justice, political freedom became the voices within me. God could not be found anywhere. Yet the voice inside me whispered, nagged about questions still unanswered. I had to confront the problem. My solution was to hit the bare minimum. Yes, I believe in God; no, the Church is not part of my belief.

In the last ten years I have come to the conviction that there is God and there are many manifestations by which God is known. I have always had trouble with Jesus Christ. I believe him to be a historical figure, but not God. The subsequent actions that follow were a rebuttal of the Church and the sacraments. I found this very hard to do. It is difficult to escape one's religious obligations, due to the force of habit and more importantly, due to the cultures in which these practices are situated.

First, I had to clarify in my mind that this was not a rebellious streak. I thought about it deeply for a long time. I do not deny God. In fact, I affirm my belief in God. However, I cannot accept an institutional Church and its empty rituals. Yet, my problem is in the fact that there is an emptiness because the physical bearings are gone. I am in the process of building my symbols.

I had a discussion with my husband about my convictions. At first, he thought it was just a phase I was going through. He tried to bring out my doubts but I had done enough investigation and introspection to know what I wanted and what I believed in. He respects my convictions because he knows that I am committed to values of justice, peace and harmony. It is my belief.

Even my children have realized some aspects of my belief in God. I have explained it to my older kids. But it was most difficult for my younger children. When my son had his first communion 2 years ago, I could not explain why I did not go to communion. I gave a white lie (is there such a thing?) about having had a meal.

Today, I join my family at mass every Sunday not because of my Sunday obligation but I feel that in some way I must give public worship within a community; it need not be a Catholic Church. I also feel that I should not influence my family to practice my beliefs. They should come to an understanding of God and religion in their lives on their own. I prick their interest and I present questions for debate, but I want them to make their own decisions.

I feel more at peace with myself. I don't think it is the end of my questioning. There is so much more to question. Part of the joy of getting older and gaining experience is that one knows more and desires to know more. One mellows. Has religion been a liberating or oppressing influence in my life? Both. At different times in my life. ⊛

Sr. Rose

"Inay! Itay! Huwag ho ninyong kalilimutan yung pasalubong ninyong puto-bumbong, bibingka at litson."

Whenever I recall my childhood I usually remember this, telling my parents, who go to Baclaran every Wednesday to attend the Novena of Mother of Perpetual Help, not to forget to buy me presents. My parents usually bring home *pasalubong* (presents) for us. And this became the key point of my longing to go to Baclaran, hear the novena and afterwards buy food. I associated these *pasalubong* with Mother of Perpetual Help. Because of this I became close to her since my childhood. I would always ask her to be with me whenever I have exams in school, when I want to ask my parents for something which I feel they might not grant, whenever there was somebody in our family who was sick and whenever there was a birthday celebrant.

All the children in our family studied in non-Catholic schools except for two of my sisters who were Scholasticans. My mother was my first "Religion teacher". She taught me how to pray the basic prayers and the rosary. My father was the one who gave me my first prayer book entitled "My Little Prayer Book". Inay would always tell me to pray before going to bed and upon waking up in the morning. She would always tell me to be good, honest and obedient especially to my elders. According to her, God loved these kinds of children. So when my first Communion Day came (I was in Grade Five) I was very happy because I knew then that I was a good child of God.

My image of God at that time was unclear. I would always pray to Mother of Perpetual Help instead of praying to our Lord Jesus Christ. I would always join my parents when they go to Baclaran and of course next on the agenda is the "puto-bumbong, bibingka, and the litson" (roasted pig).

In mid-November 1968, we stopped going to Baclaran because Itay had his first heart attack. This was the beginning
of my spiritual crisis. He was confined at the hospital for
almost a month. He was unable to recover. He closed his
eyes the following month. I thought this was the end of the
world. I could vividly recall how I talked with Mother of
Perpetual Help and to our Lord Jesus Christ. At that time, I
turned to God and asked him so many questions. Why did He
take my father away when he was so loving and responsible,
the best father in the world. I was so depressed that even my
schooling was affected.

I was very much attached to my father. I would lie down
on his lap while watching television. He would stroke my hair
until I fell asleep and he would bring me to my bed. He would
accompany me to the beauty parlor when I have my hair done
whenever I would be included in the school program. My
grade school years were meaningful, fruitful and happy years
with my father. I was the apple of his eye. He would immediately give me what I want. He would always make it a point
that all the things we needed in school were ready. He was
very concerned about our studies.

These are now memories, my childhood days with my
father which I treasure most. With these memorable experiences it took me years to accept that my father was/is with
the Lord in eternal happiness. With my father's passing Inay
became both our mother and father.

I began to get closer to Mama Mary. The image of Mama
Mary for me that time was a loving, sweet, caring and gentle
mother. I also began to pray to the Sto. Niño.

My college graduation day was my most memorable day
in college. That was the time when I received my two medals
—one for being an honor student (Cum Laude),the other was
the Leadership Award. I gave my first medal to my mother as
a sign of my love and gratitude to her. The other, I gave to my
brother for he always encouraged me to be strong in facing
challenges in life.

College was over and I faced a new life. Right after graduation I worked as a teacher in St. Scholastica's College,
Grade School Department. When my gangmates found out I
accepted the job, they started to tease me, saying that some-
day they will have a classmate a *sister* in St. Scholastica's

College, Grade School Department. I did not take this seriously. I even told them, Who? Me? A sister? *Impossible!*

So, summer came and I started to work. During my breaktime the Principal asked me if I knew of somebody who was also a teacher. I recommended my sister. She accepted her at once. Both of us started on the same year, 1976. Everything was beautiful for me that year — I graduated with honors which was my mother's dream. I had a fine job, my sister was with me.

However something was bothering me. I wanted to continue my studies. So without the knowledge of my principal I enrolled for my M.A., Saturday classes. I thought there would be conflicts with my studies and work. But there were none. After some years, I was able to finish the academic requirements. When I was about to write my thesis I stopped because of my vocation.

Retreats and prayer group sessions were parts of the Faculty Development Program then. I attended several retreats and prayer group sessions but the most striking one was in 1977 when we had Father Oggorman, SJ as our Retreat Master at the Sacred Heart Retreat House, Novaliches. I had a different feeling that pushed me to confide in him and Sr. M. Beatrice, OSB, the head of the program. I thought it was just something ordinary. However according to them, this was somethng different and I have to pray for it.

A lot of sisters came to see me. My co-teachers noticed this and started asking questions why the sisters kept talking to me. I just told them that they want something important from me. I could not reveal this to them, especially to my sister. It did not occur to them that I had an inclination to enter the convent... to become a sister. They always thought I was the outgoing type. I enjoyed parties, movies, discos.

After several months, I started airing this to my mother, sisters, brothers and even to my boyfriend. They did not approve. I was then an "obedient" child so I did not say anything.

But I felt uneasy, disturbed. I re-established my line of communication with the sisters. I was to take a lot of scheduled tests in the Formation House. I was telling myself that if I pass or fail, it's God's will. I took the exams last January

The situation ran so fast that I again aired this to my beloved mother, loving and caring sisters and brothers and to my boyfriend (who was ready to tell my mother his plan of settling down with me).

My mother scolded me for the first time in my life! My sisters and brothers told me to stop teaching. They prepared and processed my papers for England.

But on December of that year, I accepted an invitation to a Vocation Retreat. On this retreat, I made my final decision. Right after the retreat, I "eloped" with Sister M. Pauline, OSB. We went to Angeles. There I found myself at peace. It was the first time that I left my family. I welcomed the New Year with a new family... the Missionary Benedictine Sisters!

Homesickness was my greatest problem during my first three years in formation. Since I was very much attached to my family, I always received letters from them, especially from my mother who was in England that time. The more letters I received, the more I long for my mother. However my formator helped me solve this problem. Luckily, I was able to transcend this.

Because of so many struggles and conflicts, my image of God was changed to God of History and Mary the Magnificat...

> *My soul proclaims the greatness of the Lord...*
> *He has shown the strength of his arm,*
> *He has scattered the proud in their conceit.*
> *He has cast down the mighty from their thrones,*
> *And has lifted up the lowly.*
> *He has filled the hungry with good things,*
> *And the rich he has sent away empty...*

Lk 1:46-55

Now as a Junior Sister, having studied at Sisters Formation Institute, Mary Hill School of Theology and St. Scholastica's College Women's Studies, I became so open to the reality of the world. The New Heaven and the New Earth became so meaningful to me.

The emerging spirituality of women today—vibrant, liberating, colorful and wholly alive—makes my sisterhood, my being a Missionary Benedictine Sister today more relevant especially in answering the call of the signs of the times.

To end this, I would like to quote what Sister Virginia Fabella, MM wrote in her "Mission of Women in the Church in Asia: Role and Position".

> *The aim of women's liberation and struggle for equality in the church and in society is not to get even with men or to replace them as oppressors. The true end of our struggles is a more just and human society for all, a society that reflects God's kingdom of love, truth, justice and peace. But liberation will come only if we first admit we need it, only if we truly want it, only if we are willing to struggle for it with all the other women.. together.*

Once again I am looking at an Asian woman:
"She has a round face, a small nose
She has short legs
She is short in height
She is elegant and graceful."

She is the woman of Amor VI and Amor VII.
She hears a voice assuring her:
Woman, you are set free from your infirmities.

(Lk 13:12)

And immediately she straightens up and praises God. ⊗

Karla Francisco

1964. Upsurge of youth radicalism. Young men and women activists could be seen in rallies and demons-trations in Malacañang, Plaza Miranda... Kabataang Makabayan founded.

My apolitical and business-oriented clan was a mere observer of this historical event. They were in the province, preoccupied by a new-born baby. I was born during that year. Not a member of the clan disagreed when my maternal grand-father said that my looks indicate that I would be a very good follower of the Virgin Mary. I was then named after the Virgin Mary.

Although my parents were conservative, my religious upbringing was not that strict. My parents were always out of town for business.

However, since I was born, I was expected to be a good follower of the Virgin Mary and Jesus. In the family this meant having long hair, being a homebody, modest and sub-servient. As a child, I would always observe the image of Virgin Mary in our altar and find out if we physically looked the same. I would even cover my head with a white silk table cloth, and would try to look so tame. To myself, I would say, 'Hmmmnnnn... puwede na rin.'

I played the role of an angel during *Santacruzan* or *May-flower Festival*, Virgin Mary for *Panunuluyan* during Christ-mas and an angel who unveils the black cloth of Virgin Mary during Easter Sunday. But when I was asked to portray the role of Mary Magdalene in one play, I refused because I had never seen Mary Magdalene as anything but a prostitute.

I was a "saint" in the family and I loved what I consi-dered the old living saints or the nuns and the priests with whom I could feel the presence of God. I was very close to them. I would even kiss their hands as a sign of respect whenever I saw them.

I just wondered why the clergy in my town did not go to the barrio, especially to the peasants. They only went there during fiestas when there were masses. They visited only the barrio captain or the prominent families.

1970s. The youth were reading Marx. Lennon's songs and Lenin's works were their favorites. Ang Bayan Ko was heard amid rallies in Malacañang and Plaza Miranda. MAKIBAKA (Malayang Kilusan ng Bagong Kababaihan) was out to prove that women were fighting alongside men for genuine freedom. Martial Law in, democracy out. Kabataang Makabayan outlawed; Kabataang Barangay founded. Many were detained, countless were salvaged and tortured.

In entered the learning institution to praise the New Society, to be subservient to authority and to appreciate repressive and colonial education. My mind was conditioned not to understand oppression, exploitation, militarization and poverty. Miseducation imprisoned me.

In school I also learned the sexist language of the Lord's Prayer, the Ten Commandments and other religious beliefs. Critical thinking was discouraged. I learned to be thankful for poverty and suffering because "they who suffer and thirst shall receive the blessings of God." Charity work was to be done by good followers of Virgin Mary and Jesus. I always helped the victims of calamity by giving food and clothes. Oftentimes, my mother would get mad because I would even offer them my new dresses and toys. I also loved to help our less fortunate neighbors in weaving the baskets they sold to my parents so they would earn more money.

However, my image of being modest and homey like Virgin Mary faded. In my intermediate grades, I became the overall president of our school's Barangayette, the elementary version of Kabataang Barangay. I couldn't stay at home too much for I was always at inter-school meetings and activities. Barangayettes were partners of the Kabataang Barangay during the "Alay Lakad, Alay Tanim, lahat ng alay sa Bagong Lipunan."

Being exposed to other schools' pupil-leaders, I developed a crush on one of them. I sent him a love note and I would always pass in front of their house. In my excitement, I told my classmate about it. For a woman to say her feelings to a man is contrary to the norms of Philippine society (especially in the province) no matter how sincere and unmalicious she is. She will be branded as immoral and indecent.

I became the center of intrigues. The boy's mother went to our house with my teacher to talk to my parents and grandmother. I was reprimanded because, according to them, I was setting a disgusting example to other girls in our school.

I was so ashamed. I didn't know if it was a sin but I was crying when I asked the forgiveness of Virgin Mary/God for what I did. For the family, I violated the law of modesty attached to Mary. I was so guilty.

During my elementary graduation, no one in my family wanted to escort me to my graduation march. I was delivering my valedictory address and I couldn't help my tears not because I finished my elementary schooling with flying colors but because I felt I had no moral authority to speak of goodness before parents, teachers, and fellow graduates. I asked myself if I was no longer a good example of Mary's followers.

Late '70s. The students formed the Students Alliance Against Tuition Fee Increases... Student governments restored. The colonial, repressive and commercialized educational system was among the issues raised during youth and student rallies in Metro Manila. Many students died and countless were wounded during the bloody confrontations of anti-riot policemen and demonstrators.

As I was in the province, I didn't witness these. I would just scan these in the papers. Besides, I was more interested to read Nancy Drew Mysteries and Mills and Boon. Otherwise, I was busy with my slum books. I would say that the contents of my slum books somehow influenced me. When male respondents were asked questions like 'Who is your ideal woman?', the usual answer would be "Virgin Mary" and I would get thrilled. A question like 'How would you describe your ideal girl?' would be answered: "cute, charming, kind, romantic, intelligent, sexy, good cook, industrious, modest and religious."

Religiosity counted most especially in a Catholic school like mine. I was an Aglipay when I finished elementary schooling but when I reached high school and enrolled in the lone Catholic School in our town, I was converted.

Going to church, novenas, processions, confession and other religious practices became an obligation. Sometimes, I just fell asleep while reciting the prayers but I still went there to have my attendance checked so I would garner additional points for my religion class.

During my Junior and Senior Year, I became a catechist. I was to go to non-catholic schools in our town and teach the bible to the students. Unconsciously, I became an instrument to perpetuate the conservative interpretation of the Bible to the poor children of the barrio folk. I pitied the unhealthy and dirty children in the barrio but I couldn't say anything except that they should accept their poverty and oppression so they would receive the blessings of God.

My religious background influenced my plans after high school. I wanted to become a nun to complete my service to God but my mother objected. We decided on a Junior Secretarial Education. This, she said, would give me enough time to think my plan through. If my mind wouldn't change, I could still go to the nunnery but if not, there would be an assurance that I could land a job.

1981. Martial Law was lifted. After a series of militant protest actions, dialogues, pickets, lobbying, the government was forced to grant the basic rights of students to organize through student governments and campus papers.

I came to Manila. I entered the university and was greeted by protest actions against tuition fee increases and the existing educational system. On the street walls, I would see grand slogans in red paint; on campus, I would see the red banners and scattered propaganda materials, and not only once in a week were classes disrupted because of boycotts. Classes were always suspended. Everything was abstract to me. I couldn't understand the sudden change of my environment. I came from a relatively 'peaceful' Catholic school in the province. It was a culture shock. I wanted to ask a lot of questions by my college professors were politically deaf, blind and mute. My classmates, like me, were a bunch of mis-educated and politically unaware students. I tried to read some of the leaflets but I couldn't understand the meaning of the US-Marcos love team although I saw them on the street walls. For me, it was easier to understand the Sharon-Gabby love team which I always saw on movie billboards. And my! I couldn't take the other words in the leaflets. They were full of anger toward the government, school administrations, etc. For me, it was against my religious background. These were against God!

Whenever I had a feeling of internal contradiction, I was trained to go to the church. In the university, the nearest place to go to was the school chapel. I asked for serenity from God and I prayed for the boycotters that they may realize how sinful their acts were.

Later on, I became a member of the Charismatic Fellowship hoping to find some answers. But while singing songs and uttering prayers, swaying hands and dancing while praising the Greatest One to the fullest, I couldn't feel its significance, not because I didn't know how to dance or sing, but I felt it didn't answer my questions and the contradictions within me.

When the university administration was forced to establish the student council I found a new venue where I could continue my search. I became an officer of the University Student Council. I started to join teach-ins, discussion groups, room-to-room campaigns, boycotts, pickets, etc. I was too slow in recognizing the -isms of society but I could sense that it partially answered my multifarious questions. Nevertheless, politics and religion left me with unresolved contradictions.

1983. Ninoy Aquino was assassinated. Yellow fever came in. The Filipino people realized the evil of dictatorial government. Former President Marcos deployed secret marshalls to eye the suspected subversives.

I graduated from Secretarial Education. I no longer wanted to be a nun although I could feel that my commitment to serve God and the people was still in my heart. I studied Political Science. I was lucky to have progressive and nationalist professors who contributed much in strengthening my theoretical foundation. They exposed me to various ideas including Theology of Liberation. In the beginning theories were so difficult to absorb. But reality proved the correctness of theories. My exposure and integration with the masses deepened my political involvement. I could already contextualize the bible in the present situation. The people's movement would remind me of the Jesus movement.

I was no longer a mere listener or spectator. I became a mobilizer, organizer and speaker.

"If you deviate from the prevailing norms, you're branded as immoral, indecent and subversive." I experienced this as a result of the liberation I attained. For the second time in my life, I created another controversy in our clan. They couldn't believe that I was an activist. The elders in my clan accepted that they were wrong when they said I would be a good follower of Virgin Mary and Jesus. I often experienced being slapped by my parents and being locked in my room, so I couldn't attend my political activities (fortunately, I always escaped through the window or roof). Also, I was isolated from every young member of our clan because my tongue, the elders said, will spread a contagious virus, speaking of Godless ideas, thus, subversion. For them, I caused dishonor because activism was taboo in our family.

1986. The US-Marcos Dictatorship was toppled down by people's power. The Cory Aquino government came in. Massacres salvagings, saturation drives, raids, vigilantes, peso devaluation, oil price hike. Nothing substantial happened.

Amidst the economic and political crises, I was still in the forefront of the people's struggle. Feminism was added to my dictionary. When I see women in the picketlines, demonstrations and rallies, when I see women willing to sacrifice their lives for their commitment and faith to serve God's children, I remember the active participation of women in the Jesus movement.

Today, I am close to church people. Some of them don't even have churches anymore; they were denied by their superiors because of their political involvement. For me, they are the true representatives of Christ. They, who are not afraid to talk about genuine liberation. I do not kiss their hands anymore. Instead, I link arms with them to fight oppression. More so, I could feel God's spirit in the determination of the masses, women and men fighting for a more humane world.

Today, I tell my family that I am still a good follower of the Virgin Mary and Jesus, but like them, I put myself in the present context of our society.

rituals
for women

MORNING WORSHIP
IN GOD'S IMAGE

Sr. Virginia Fabella, MM

Leader: Let us place ourselves in the presence of our loving and gracious God our Creator who has made each of us to reflect the beauty, compassion, and wisdom of the God-head.

All: Blessed and praised be the good and compassionate One who has created us in God's image.

Leader: This morning we are gathered to celebrate our humanity which God has fashioned to enjoy and receive the abundance of creation for God's glory and life's fullness.

All: Blessed and praised be the good and the compassionate One who has created us in God's image.

Leader: Let us begin our praise by praying Psalm 8 together:

All: O God, our God,
how glorious is your name over all the earth!
You have exalted your majesty above the heavens.
Out of the mouths of babes and suckling you have
fashioned praise... to silence the hostile and the
vengeful.
When I behold your heavens, the work of your fingers
the moon and the stars which you set in place —
Who are we that you should be mindful of us,
that you should care for us?
You have made us little less than the gods
and crowned us with glory and honor.
You have given us rules over the works of your hands,
putting all things under our feet:
All sheep and oxen, yes, and the beasts of the field,
the birds of the air, the fishes of the sea
and whatever swims the paths of the seas.
God, our God, how glorious is your name
over all the earth!

Leader: Throughout human history, there have been many

interpretations of how man and woman come to be, which have become parts of national folktales and myths. Here we want to share two readings. The first is a Philippine legend which portrays the beginnings of the first man and woman, characterized by mutuality and equality. The second reading is found in Genesis.

Reader 1: One day the ruler among birds, the *tikling,* flew, its wings flapping into the vast skies. Over the trees, it flew in a wide embracing circle. It was a white bird with glistening white feathers. From afar, the bird saw a tall bamboo on which to rest. The bird pecked and pecked at a bamboo stalk until it split open, and out stepped together into life, hand in hand, equal and bound to each other by a common nature and a simultaneous emergence, the man called *Malakas* (the strong) and the woman *Maganda* (the beautiful). (Pause.)

Reader 2: Then God said, "Let us make humanity in our image, after our likeness; and let them have dominion over the fish of the sea, and over the birds of the air, and over the cattle, and over all the earth, and over every creeping thing that creeps upon the earth." So God created humanity in God's own image, in the image of God was humanity created; male and female God created them. And God blessed them, and said to them, "Be fruitful and multiply, and fill the earth and subdue it; and have dominion over the fish of the sea and over the birds of the air and over every living thing that moves upon the earth."

Leader: Let us pause for a minute to reflect on this Scriptural passage as we play a Filipino song, Kalayaan.

Kalayaan. Freedom. To be free is one of the many gifts that likens us to the divine. It is out of God's freedom and love that we have been called to being.

Freedom is precious. We struggle to regain it when it has been taken away, we purify it when it has been defaced, we strive to remain in freedom to be faithful to the divine image.

As we listen to Kalayaan, let each of us say in a word or phrase what being created in God's image means for us as women.

Music: Kalayaan

Leader: Now, let our voices become one in praying for a new world where God's image in both women and men is respected:

Reader 3: Our gracious Father-Mother, may "we look forward to the age of peace, when violence is banished, where both women and men are able to love and be loved, and the work and wealth of our world is justly shared."

All: We pray to you, hear our prayer.

Reader 4: May "all the forces for good, love, peace and justice, all the creative powers of the universe work with us to achieve that vision."

All: We pray to you, hear our prayer.

Reader 5: Help us to "take our stand on the solidarity of humanity, the oneness of life, and the unnaturalness and injustice of all special favoritism, whether of gender, race or country."

All: We pray to you, hear our prayer.

Reader 6: May women unite to strengthen relationships built on equality not subordination.

All: We pray to you, hear our prayer.

Leader: Let us conclude our worship with an affirmation of our belief in ourselves as women challenged to work for the transformation of the world into one that truly depicts humanity as the image of God.

All: We are women. We are Asian. We are alive. We are struggling. We are hoping.

We are created in the image of God just like all other people in the world. We are persons of worth and dignity. We are thinking persons, feeling persons, and doing persons. Each of us is a small "I am" that stands before the big "I AM". We are workers who are constantly challenged and faced with the needs of the church and society in Asia and in the global community.

We are angered by the structures of power that create all forms of oppression, exploitation and degradation. We are witnesses to the moans and tears, banners and clenched fists of our people. We can hear their liberating songs, their hopeful prayers and decisive march toward justice and freedom. We believe that all of us—women and men, young and old, Christian and non-Christian—are called upon to do responsible action, to be concerned, to be involved NOW! We are hoping. We are struggling. We are alive. We are Asian. We are women. 🞜

CELEBRATING A WOMEN'S BOOK
(Adapted from rituals in *Churches in Solidarity with Women*, a publication of the World Council of Churches.)
Sr. Mary Bellarmine Bernas, OSB

Women's Creed
(adapted from Rachel C. Wahlberg)

I believe in God
who created woman and man
in God's own image
who created the world
and gave both sexes
the care of the earth.

I believe in Jesus
child of God
born of the woman Mary
who listened to women and liked them
who stayed in their homes
who discussed the Kingdom with them
who was followed and financed
by women disciples.

I believe in Jesus
who discussed theology with a woman
at a well
and first confided in her
his messiahship
who motivated her to go and tell
her great news to the city.

I believe in Jesus who received anointing
from a woman at Simon's house
who rebuked the men guests
who scorned her.

Ritual for launching of *Essays on Women* held last August 27, 1987 at Maryville, St. Scholastica's College, Manila.

I believe in Jesus
who said this woman will be remembered
for what she did —
minister for Jesus.

I believe in Jesus
who thought of pregnancy and birth
with reverence
not as punishment — but
as wrenching event
a metaphor for transformation
born again
anguish-into-joy.

I believe in the wholeness
of the Saviour
in whom there is neither
Jew nor Greek
slave nor free
male nor female
for we are all one
in salvation.

I believe in the Holy Spirit
the woman spirit of God
who like a hen
created us
and gave us birth
and covers us
with her wings.

A Litany of Woman's Power
(adapted from Ann M. Heidkamp)

Sister Mary Bellarmine (SMB): Spirit of life, we remember today the women, named and unnamed, who throughout time have used the power and gifts you gave them to change the world. We call upon these foremothers to help us discover within ourselves your power—and the ways to use it to bring about the Kingdom of Justice and Peace in our country.

SMB: We remember SARAH who with Abraham answered God's call to forsake her homeland and put their faith in a covenant with the Lord.

All: We pray for her power and faith:

SMB: We remember ESTHER and DEBORAH, who by acts of individual courage saved their nation.

All: We pray for their power and courage to act for the greater good.

SMB: We remember MARY MAGDALENE, and the other women who followed Jesus who were disbelieved when they announced the resurrection.

All: We pray for their power of belief in the face of skepticism.

SMB: We remember TERESA of Avila and CATHERINE of Siena who challenged the corruption of the Church during the Renaissance.

All: We pray for their powers of intelligence and outspokenness.

SMB: We remember our own MOTHERS and GRANDMOTHERS whose lives shaped ours. We remember our great women GABRIELA SILANG, TANDANG SORA, and the heroic WOMEN OF MALOLOS whose lives are shining examples for Filipinas of all time.

All: We pray for their power of leadership and compassion.

SMB: We remember the women of today who contribute their work tirelessly in their fields, SR. MARY JOHN, OSB and the authors of the book we are launching today, as well as other women whose talents and achievements have remained unrecognized.

All: We pray for their power to persevere and open new possibilities for all women.

SMB: We remember the women in our country who face a life of poverty, who are victims of violence in their homes, and are discriminated in society.

All: We pray for their power of hopefulness to work together for a better life.

SMB: We remember our daughters and all young Filipinas, the bearers of hope and promise in our mother land.

All: We pray for their power to seek the fullness of life and salvation.

SMB: We have celebrated the power of many women past and present. It is now time to celebrate ourselves. Within each of us lies the seeds of power and glory. Our bodies can touch with love, our hearts can heal, our minds can seek out faith and truth and justice. Spirit of life, be with us in our quest. Amen. ✾

A RITUAL OF COMPLETION
AND SEPARATION
(Adapted from Florence Perella Hayes, Chaplain at McGill
University, Montreal, Canada)

Marjorie M. Evasco

*This ritual is a product of communal experience,
having been inspired by the work of Florence Hayes and the
words and gestures of many other women friends. It expresses a shared human need, as women must feel it, to
wield the power of closure in human relationships, to bring
broken pieces together in life's great mosaic, to create a
sense of wholeness in the face of fragmentation, and to view
endings not as a shattering but as another way of gathering
whatever is enduring to the essential self.*

*This ritual was never performed but its writing was an
exercise of woman's will which was complete unto itself.*

Participants: The couple and two friends who join them
in reading the service
The children
Other close relatives and friends

Symbols: A large goblet filled to the top with wine; A
bowl of earth; a plate of salt; a flask of vinegar,
2 red roses for each child

Gestures:
I. Greetings and Invocation
II. Remembering the Vision
III. Darkening of the Vision
XV. Healing
V. Reaffirming Parenthood
VI. Returning to Origins
VII. Blessing

(Each of the 7 steps begins with an appropriate reading from
Scripture or poetry or song, and each concludes with a few
moments of silence before moving on.)

Greetings and Invocation

Woman's Best Friend (WBF): Welcome to all who have been drawn here out of love for (names of man and woman). We, their family and friends, join them today to mark the completion of their married life, and to ask the Great Spirit to bless them as they face the challenge of a new journey. May the Great Spirit grace them now and with loving kindness in the days to come.

Man's Best Friend (MBF): "Now the earth was a formless void, there was darkness ever the deep, and God's spirit hovered over the waters. God said 'Let there be light,' and there was light. God saw that light was good and God divided light from darkness." (Gen. 1:1-4.)

WBF: Falling in love is a bolt of divine knowledge, and a crack of light in the darkness.

MBF: Falling in love is the light of seeing together towards the same direction.

She & He: We honor that vision we once shared and the good work of our life together.

She & He: (Each, in turn, names a positive memory or a satisfying work done together.)

She & He: To affirm these things and bond them to our hearts forever, we drink from this common cup. (Each tastes from the cup.)

Darkening of the Vision

WBF: Opposite female, stands male,
opposite life, death,
opposite light, darkness,
yin and yang. This is the way to view
all the works of the Holy One; they go in
mutual pairs.

She: Love once called us together,
now life demands our separation.

In sorrow I accept the ways by which
we have grown differently.

He: In sorrow I accept my fears
and the dishonesty in which I hid.

She: In sorrow I accept the different ways by which
we see
> ourselves,
> each other,
> our world

He: In sorrow I accept the ways
I used these differences against you
instead of accepting and understanding
> myself,
> you,
> our world.

She & He: Accept my sorrow and remember it with kindness.

(Everyone in silence passes the plate of salt and flask of vinegar and tastes both salt and vinegar.)

Healing

WBF: "There is a season for everything, a time for every occupation under heaven:

a time for giving birth;
a time for dying;
a time for planting;
a time for uprooting what has been planted."
> (Ecclesiastes 3:1-2)

She: There was time to link our lives together
and there is a time to sever.

He: What is holy about separation?
What is holy about the ending of a dream?

MBF: It is the holiness of letting go,
and of admitting there is no one and
nothing we possess.

WBF: It is the holiness of blessing
one another's freedom.
It is the refusal to consume and destroy
the one we once desired.

She & He: It is to accept our just limits.
As the remainder of this cup is emptied,
the remainder of our marriage is poured out
    upon the good earth.

(Together, they pour some wine onto the earth.)

Reaffirming Parenthood

WBF: "Your children sit round your table like shoots around the olive tree." (Ps. 128:36).

She: Love continued the work of the Great Spirit's
creation in us. We honor these new persons,
our children, (names of children)
who now grace us,
    challenge us,
    and extend our horizons.

He: They are the enfleshment of the love
we shared; the wonder and the joy,
the consolation and the anguish of our lives.
I affirm my commitment to them as
long as I live.

She: We continue to be parents and children even when we no longer are husband and wife. As a sign of the covenant of parenthood, we share this final taste of our common cup.

(Parents and children all taste from the cup of wine, leaving some at the bottom. Each parent gives each child a red rose.)

Returning to Origins

WBF: *Who are you? What have you done?*
A name should be an expression of our essential selves. That name may be revealed to us slowly in the process of our lives. It may be spoken by others after we die, or it may remain forever hidden with God.

MBF: *Where have you come from? Where are you going?*
In the meantime, we wear a public name, infuse it and shape it, a key for those who care and a mystery to all others.

She: To mark the completion of our old lives together, sharing lives, sharing names

I give you back this ring
because the sacred round of our togetherness
has been transgressed;

I give you back this cord
because the sacred ties of our kinship
have been cut;

I give you back this arrae
because our common wealth and substance
have become impoverished;

I give you back this veil
because the sacred veil of our love's sanctuary
has been torn in half;

I give you back these candles
because the light of our vision has been darkened
by our looking into divergent directions;

I give you back these vestments of our marriage
because its purity has been tainted;

and because you have deliberately withheld
nurture to what I freely gave of myself.

I take back my name,
I assert full claims upon my body,
I take with me the children I have
borne with this body,
I take back my spirit,
I take back my soul,

and choose to live complete unto myself.

He: We have reached the point where we once
began.
The full circle is complete;
I respect your affirmation of your separate being,
just as I respect my own.
As you prepare to heal on your own,
I, too, shall take full responsibility
for my own healing and growth.

May this true completion
of sixteen years of a life together
allow us to heal and recognize the good
we have done.

Blessing

(All lift hands to bless the pair. They may simply receive the blessing or they may lift hands to bless one another.)

MBF: We lift our hands in blessing to (names of children)

May they find the strength and courage to forge their individual lives in serenity and good health.

WBF: May they be deeply familiar with satisfying good work, true friendship, and their children's love.

All: May they grow in the wisdom and breath of God.

(Each family member and friend goes to the woman and man, and to the children and makes a personal gesture of blessing, such as resting hands upon shoulders, an embrace, a kiss.)◲

Florence Perrella Hayes, "A Ritual of Divorce," *Women Church: Theology and Practice of Feminist Liturgical Communities* by Rosemary Radford Ruether, 1985. New York: Harper and Row Publishers, Inc.

RE-DEDICATION AND HEALING OF A HOUSE AFTER DIVISION AND DEEP PAIN

(Adapted from Rosemary Radford Reuther)

Marjorie M. Evasco

Participants: Members of the household
Close friends and relatives

Symbols: Candles, blessed water, branches of fragrant plants, incense, food and wine

Gestures: I. Greeting and Invocation
II. Naming the Vision and the Violation
III. Affirmation of Love, Strength, and Wisdom
IV. Blessing the House and Dedication
V. Gathering of Kindred

(The ritual begins with the persons who live in the house standing at the center, together with the priestess and friends.)

Greeting and Invocation

Priestess: Welcome to all who have been drawn here out of love for (names of mother, daughter and son). We, their family and friends, join them today in re-dedicating and healing their house, and to ask God's blessings upon them as they face the new challenges of their lives together. May the Holy One grace them now and with loving kindness in the days to come.

Naming the Vision and Violation

Mother: This house is our home, the place of our rest and our security. We have looked forward to return to this house so many times to find the place where we rest, seek shelter and security. This, our house, had been violated. Instead of a place of security and peace, it became a place of dread, anger and sorrow. Its integrity had been broken, its peace shattered.

Priestess: A reading from the prophet Isaiah 24:4-12.

The earth dries up and withers: the whole world grows weak; both earth and sky decay. The people have defiled the earth by breaking God's laws and by violating the covenant made to last forever...

The city of chaos is broken down, every house is shut up so none can enter. Desolation is left in the city; the gates are battered into ruins.

Affirmation of Love, Strength and Wisdom

Son: We will not submit to fear, anger and pain. Holy Wisdom is our strength and protection.

Daughter: We will once more make this house into a home, a place of security, peace and love. We will go on living here, drawing strength and protection from our mutual love.

Mother: We now put a closure to the sad and painful events that took place in this house. These difficult moment need not be forgotten, but we will not let them control our future. We carry with us the good memories, drawing strength from them.

All members of the household: This, our house, we transform into a home, a place of peace, security and love. Let it be a place of joy, of fruitful work, refreshing rest, and strengthening ties with those we love.

Blessing and Dedication

(Led by the priestess and household members, the group circles first the garden, some bearing fragrant branches, one carrying a pot of lighted incense. The mother traces a furrow unto the earth with a stick and the children leave a trail of grain in this furrow to symbolize the circle of life. They pause a while to recite the invocation.)

All: The peace and security of Holy Wisdom and good friends surround this house and guard it from all evil.

(The group enters the house. They light their candles. They go from door to door, window to window and recite the blessing.)

All: The peace and security of Holy Wisdom and good

friends secure these doors and these windows and keep all evil from entering here.

(The group goes to each part of the house and all the good possible activities in the rooms are evoked.)

Daughter: In this sala, let the space be filled with welcoming warmth and kindness for friends and strangers alike, who grace us with their presence. Let the members of this home who spend time in this space enjoy good things together: music, conversation, laughter, tv shows.

Son: In this kitchen, let the space be filled with laughter and good conversation. Let the smell of fragrant dishes arise from the stove. Let the work of this kitchen be shared by all who partake of its good things. May our bodies and spirits be nourished into health and strength by its produce.

Other members of the household: In this laundry area and the bathrooms of this house, may our bodies be cleansed of all physical, mental, and spiritual pollution and may we be freed of dirt and exhaustion that we may work and rest re-energized and purified.

Mother: In this main bedroom, let the space fill with peace and well-being. Let the quiet activities of studying, writing, and storytelling flow into the well-earned sleep for the night. Let the persons who rest here find strength as they dream and prepare themselves for another day's good work at school and at the office.

Other members of the household: In this second bedroom, let the space fill with serenity and careful sharing. Let sleep recharge the bodies, minds, and spirits of the persons who use this space.

(After the invocation of the good spirits of each room, blessed water is sprinkled by the priestess throughout the rooms.)

Gathering of Kindred

(The ritual concludes with the group gathering at the table laden with food. The incense pot is placed at the center, with the fragrant branches put in a vase.)

All: (with hands joined)
    In the power of Holy Wisdom, we join together to be

strength and protection for each other. Let that power and strength flow from hand to hand, from touch to touch, glance to glance, word to word.

Let us bind up the wounds of this house and each others' wounds.

Peace and love be with us all.

(Everyone share the food and the wine.) ⌘

A PRAYER FOR EMPOWERMENT

Pia Crisostomo Arboleda

Hail Powerful Queen, Mother of Courage
Hail our life, our strength, our hope.
To you do we protest,
   raging and weeping.
Look upon us, your children
   We, who are oppressed
     in this valley of tears.
   Our aggressors agitate the fight
     between sister and sister;
   they break our backs
     and treat us like animals;
   they fragment our bodies
     and let our children go hungry;
   they take away our souls
     and watch slowly as we die.

Turn You, Most Gracious Advocate,
Your blessings of courage upon us.
Break this bondage of silence,
   our slavery.
After this our exile
Show unto us the Power that nurtures
   the fruit of your womb.
May we stand undefeated before our enemies.
May we draw strength from you,
   O fearless, invincible One. ✿

(adapted from Hail Holy Queen)

RITUAL OF HONING WEAPONS
FOR HEALING*
(Adapted from *A Litany of Women's Power*
by Ann M. Heidkamp)
Lina Sagaral Reyes

Invocation:

Lina: Bless me, mother, for I am your child.
Bless be my eyes, that I may see your path.
Bless be my nose, that I may breathe your essence.
Bless be my mouth, that I may speak of you.
Bless be my breasts, that I may be faithful in my work.
Bless be my loins which bring forth the life of women
     and men as you bring forth all creation.
Bless be my feet, that I may walk your ways.
(Erica Jong, Witches)

Celebration of Re-membering Women's Power

All: Spirit of Life, we remember today the women, named
and unnamed, who throughout time have used the power and
gifts you have given them to change the world. We call upon
these foremothers to help us discover within ourselves your
power and the ways to use it to bring about Justice and Peace
on earth.

We remember
EVE and all the NO-NAME-WOMEN in the world's scriptures
who dared to defy the arrogance of gods who denied them
their humanity.

---

*On April 6, 1987, I celebrated the birthing of Honing Weapons, a sheaf of
14 poems. In the company of friends — there were 32 — I sent the little book
to the world through this ritual. The ritual wasn't only for the book, though. I
wrote it with a subtext of healing—like the process of making the book, the
ritual marked my own psychic and physical "honing," of willing myself well.
Yes, I believe words, spells and incantations have magic. Language
empowered me to will myself alive and well. — Lina

We accept
their heritage of god-daring and god-defying.

We remember
ENHEDUANNA who worshipped the moon
SAPPHO who praised the beauty of women
LEONA FLORENTINO who chose poetry and solitude.

We accept
their heritage of song, poetry and solitude.

We remember
TRANQUILINA MENDEZ REYES
and FRANCISCA APALISOK SAGARAL
who bequeathed Lina with their names, stories and
mother-roots.

We accept
the heritage of our mothers who birthed and named us
and first taught us mother-language.

We remember
PHOOLAN DEVI, HUA MU LAN, WINNIE MANDELA
and LORENA BARROS
for using their arms not only to embrace
but also to protect and defend thoughts and beliefs,
and those which are of value and importance to their lives.

We accept
their activism, their commitment and their capacity
to take the warrior's stance in the midst of a world
that maims and kills women, children, the poor, the aged,
the handicapped and the colored.

We remember
WOMEN ALL OVER THE WORLD in the houses, fields,
factories, streets, churches, schools, hospitals, courtrooms,
markets, laboratories, space shuttles—
who conquer with the passion for their work
the everyday burden of routine and yet continue
to explore mountains, unmarked space and unknown time.

We accept
their dreaming, even as we dream and fulfill our dreams of
being in places we've never been before, of doing things we
never could before, of daring things we never would before.

Marj: We have celebrated the power of women past and present. It is time now to celebrate ourselves. Within each of us is that same life and light and love. Within each of us lie the seeds of power and glory. Our bodies can touch with love, our hands and hearts can heal; our minds can seek out faith, truth and justice. Together, we cannot only make change, we can make a real difference.

(Each of the following friends are asked to meditate for a few moments of silence a metaphor for healing and the way towards healing.

MARJORIE EVASCO, GRACE MONTE DE RAMOS, FANNY H.B. LLEGO, ALLAN RIVAS, JUDY FREYA SIBAYAN, CIELO GABRIEL, PIA CRISOSTOMO ARBOLEDA, ROLAND TOLEN-TINO, AIDA OMOSO, JUANIYO ARCELLANA, BOY PERNIA, RAYMUND ABOG, JOY ABRENICA.)

Consecration and Thanksgiving

Marj: Spirit of Life, today as we celebrate the birthing of Lina's book, a weapon towards her own healing as well as ours, we consecrate our gifts to you and give you thanks.

All: We give you thanks for
the gift of friendship
in the women and men we have found
and who have found us;

the gift of naming
in the language that affirms our power and humanity;

the gift of re-visioning the world
with new-and-many eyes, ears, nose, skin, tongue,
limbs and guts;

and the gift of creation
  in the earth that nourishes us
  in the art that fulfills us
  in the struggle that unites us
  in the daughters and sons
  who will carry our weapons and visions
  and enrich them with their own.

(And now, we may all kiss the new mother and welcome her first-born.) ☙

COVENANT CELEBRATION FOR WICCA*
affirming a common world-vision held by creative women

Women Involved in Creating Cultural Alternatives

Grace: Today, we rejoice over this gathering of creative women. We have dreamed of such a gathering in order to create a new community of women who write. WICCA, a writer's organization composed of women now takes this occasion to declare its terms of being. WICCA stands for *Writers Involved in Creating Cultural Alternatives.* As writers, we believe that our creative work can carry the seeds of humanizing alternatives of life. As activists, we believe that these seeds must be nurtured in our daily struggles as women in order to bring forth the social transformation we envision.

Fanny: May we then invite the creative writers here today, who have started to write consciously as women, and who share the vision of a world where human powers and responsibilities are equally shared, to participate in the reading of the self-blessing ritual, as a formal declaration of their intention and commitment to be part of WICCA. Please come forward and join the ritual circle.

Self-Blessing Ritual: The Seven Powers of Self-Determination

(Salt crystals in a glass bowl is passed around from woman-to woman. Each woman takes a pinch of salt and places the crystals in her left palm. Everyone waits for the bowl of salt to come full circle. The blessings are read in unison. As each blessing is invoked, every woman puts some salt unto her tongue and with her right hand, touches the part of her body invoked in the blessing.)

---

*Adapted from Kate Pravera, "Rite of Naming." in *Women-Church* by Rosemary Ruether.

This was read during the booklaunching of *Ani*'s feminist issue held March 4, 1988 at the Museo ng Kalinangang Pilipino.

All: In blessing our foreheads
We claim the powers of reason.

In blessing our eyes
We claim the power of vision, to see clearly
the forces of life and death in our midst.

In blessing our lips
We claim the power to speak the truth
about our experiences:
We claim the power to name.

In blessing our hands
We claim our powers as artisans of a new humanity.

In blessing our wombs
We claim the power to give birth, as well as
the power to choose not to give birth.

In blessing our feet
We claim the power to walk the paths of our courageous
foremothers, and when necessary to forge new paths.

(All join palms)

In blessing each other,
We claim the power that rests collectively in our shared
struggle as women.

Blessing the Earth

(An earthen pot with soil is passed around and each woman
takes some and holds it in her right fist.)

All: We bless the earth in all its fruitfulness. In so doing, we
claim the powers of life that rest in the earth. In touch-
ing the soil we feel the energy of all who struggle this day
to rise from their oppression.

We remember those who work the land in every corner of
the earth, from Southeast Asia to Central America, they
rank among the most exploited of all the earth's peoples.

We affirm hope. There is a movement of energy across
the face of this earth which refuses to die. We claim the
collective power that is ours!

Let us rejoice today for WICCA and the work we have to do towards fulfilling our vision as writers.

(The earthen pot is passed around again and the women return their handful of earth to signify their investment of self and their commitment to the women's collective of creative writers.) 🞯

REMEMBERING AND BEQUEST *

Lina Sagaral Reyes
and Raymund Jose M. Abog

Song to open the rites

Awit ng Isang Ina
Patrick Lopez

Dugo at pawis and puhunan
Nang iluwal ang sanggol
Kaya't di tutugot
Hanggang maidulot
Ang bukas na ligtas sa salot.

Tahan na anak ko, tahan na
Nagsisikip ang dibdib ng iyong ina
Mga kamay ko'y masdan
Para sa iyo ay sugatan
Paglilinis ng marumi ng ilan.

Pakinggan mo ang daing ng bayan
Sinisiil ng sakim na iilan
Kalayaa'y ginapos,
Mamamaya'y nagpupuyos
Ang sigaw, pagbabagong lubos.

Dugo at pawis ang puhunan
Upang ipagtanggol ang sanggol
Mga kamay na laan
Umaloy sa duyan
Matututong lumaban para sa bayan.

Matututong lumaban para sa bayan.

A ritual celebrated on the occasion of the launching of the IBON Ekono-komiks special issue on women, Manila Film Center, Tanghalang Severino Reyes, Sunday, 6 March 1988, 5:00-7:00 P.M.

* Adapted from *Women-Church: Theology and Practice of Feminist Liturgical Communities* by Rosemary Ruether, 1985, New York: Harper and Row Publishers, Inc.

Opening Prayer - Sr. Mary John Mananzan

Remembering the Victims

Marjorie Evasco: Repeat the syllables until the lesson is drummed along the arteries.

All: Margaret Jones, midwife, hanged 1648; Joan Peterson, veterinarian, hanged, 1652; Isobel Insch Taylor, herbalist, burned, 1618; Mother Labeland, healer, burned, 1645; Maria Walburger Rung, burned alive, age 22, 1723; Sister Maria Reanta Sanger, subprioress, accused of being lesbian, the document certifying her torture is inscribed with the seal of the Jesuits and the words *Ad Majorem Dei Gloriam* (To the Greater Glory of God); and a million nameless women burned because they were accused as witches.

What have they done to you...

Marjorie Evasco: Repeat the syllables before the lesson hemorrhages through the brain.

All: Anna Rausch, burned, 1628, 12 years old; Sybille Lutz, burned 1628, 12 years old; Agnes Webster, drowned while her young son was forced to watch her trial by water, 1567; Veronica Zerritsch, compelled to dance in the warm ashes of her executed mother then burned alive herself, 1754, 12 years old; Sr. Maura Clarke, Dorothy Kazel, Jean Donovan, Ita Ford, martyrs of El Salvador.

What have they done to us...

Marjorie Evasco: Repeat the syllables before the lesson perforates the womb.

All: (text is read faster) Gabriela Silang, tried for rebellion and hanged, 1897; Lorena Barros, killed by government soldiers, 1976, 28 years old; Babeth Prudencio, human rights worker, seven-month pregnant, killed by government soldiers, 1987, 22 years old; Marlyn Negro, 38, farmer, beheaded by the Alsa Masa, 1987; Cecita Udtohan, 36, farmer, seven-month pregnant, stabbed, 1987; Editha Cesaba, 40, farmer, stabbed 29 times by the Alsa Masa, 1987; Sr. Vivian Beromal, killed by an anti-communist group, 29 years old, January 1988; Fely Giangan, 28, farmer, killed and burned by the Tadtads; Lisa Bolando, protest activist, 1971; Liliosa Hilao, April 6, 1973; Catalia Cristina, Leticia Celestino

1984: Soledad Salvador, Resteta Fernandez, Bakun martyrs, 1985; and other women guerillas and the hundreds of Filipinas without names nor memory who have died in the protracted war for national liberation.

What have they done to you...
What have they done to us...
What have they done...

Chorus:
Weep, O my sisters
Weep for the blood of women shed for you,
the blood of the matriarch.
the blood of the prophet,
the priestess, the witch, the revolutionary
Weep for the women slaughtered
Weep for the lovers raped
Weep for the daughters stolen,
the mothers humbled and enslaved
Weep for the sisters burned
Ad Majorem Dei Gloriam
Weep O my sisters,
weep until we rise in blood and flame
to redress and rebirth

Chorus:
We can rise with the fire of freedom
Truth is the fire that burns our chains
And we can stop the fires of destruction
Healing is a fire running through our veins

Remembering the Survivors

Lucia Pavia Ticzon: "Because who would believe the fantastic and terrible story of all of our survival those who never meant to survive?"

Reader 1: "Lean's death pains me as his wife, comrade and friend. The situation has not changed. It still is as it was in Marcos time. Cory said before that justice for Ninoy cannot be had and I'm reminding her that, because the situation has not changed. I, too, cannot hope for justice during these times. But they should have given Lean a little more time to know and remember how good a father, husband and man he is."
—Lidy Nacpil-Alejandro, GABRIELA's first secretary-general and wife of slain BAYAN leader Lean Alejandro.

Reader 2: "My grief and condolence to Liddy. The Cory government is just wasting time merely setting up investigating committees. It's been five years (since Bobby was murdered). Yayo, our child, is already seven years old." --Sylvia de la Paz, secretary-general of the Medical Action Group, wife of slain Dr. Bobby de la Paz.

Reader 3: "It hurts to lose a child. Ed was our only son. Before he was killed, he was already very concerned about the poor. In Sampaloc where he noticed many squatter areas, he would ask, "Mommy, why are there many slum dwellers here?" He was only in the first year of high school then. During vacations, he would go to farms and slums. As a mother, I actually groomed him for business. But when he said he can help more people in some other ways, I gave him still my support. He left in 1972 so that the military will not bother us. He said, "I think I have to leave the house because they are already looking for me." After 12 years, we learned of his death. September 21, 1982 in Davao. He was tortured." —Josefa Jopson, chairperson of Mother and Relatives Against Tyranny (MARTYR), mother of slain student activist Edgar Jopson.

Reader 4: "It's regret I'm feeling. We have so many dreams to accomplish together. Not only for us, but also for others. Now that he is gone, I have to double my effort. I'm pregnant. I go through fits of depression. But I think I'm still needed. I'm also another life. Liddy has a six month-old baby. She can overcome, I will too." —Fatima Sibal, wife of slain UP professor Dante Sibal during the ambush try to Dante Buscayno.

Reader 5: "Lean's death was an ugly replay of what happened to our sons and husbands. The enemies will continue to squeeze our blood up to the last drop. In the beginning, I did not like my son to join the movement. But now, here I am sharing with you. After the toppling of the strongman, we were hoping that we can find the missing persons during Marcos time. There were 666 victims of involuntary disappearances then and the Aquino government gave us 93. A congressman asked, "Would you like us to pass a law to protect displaced families?" But I was hoping there would be no more replays of what happened. —Cecilia Lagman, chairperson of Families of Victims of Involuntary Disappearances (FIND), mother of missing labor lawyer Hermon Lagman.

A Poetry Reading

I Give You Back
Joy Harjo

I release you, my beautiful and terrible
fear. I release you. You were my beloved
and hated twin, but now, I don't know you
as myself. I release you with all the
pain I would know at the death of
my daughters.

You are not my blood anymore.

I give you back to the white soldiers
who burned down my home, beheaded my children,
raped and sodomized my brothers and sisters.
I give you back to those who stole the
food from our plates when we were starving.

I release you, fear, because you hold
these scenes in front of me and I was born
with eyes that can never close.

I release you, fear, so you can no longer
keep me naked and frozen in the winter,
or smothered under blankets in the summer.

I release you
I release you
I release you
I release you

I am not afraid to be angry.
I am not afraid to rejoice.
I am not afraid to be black.
I am not afraid to be white.
I am not afraid to be hungry.
I am not afraid to be full.
I am not afraid to be hated.
I am not afraid to be loved
to be loved, to be loved, fear.

Oh, you have choked me, but I gave you the leash.
You have gutted me but I gave you the knife.
You have devoured me, but I laid myself across the fire.

I take myself back, fear.
You are not my shadow any longer.
I won't hold you in my hands.

You can't live in my eyes, my ears, my voice
my belly, or in my heart my heart
my heart my heart

But come here, fear
I am alive and you are so afraid of dying.

Prayer of Intercessions

Sr. Mary John Mananzan: Let us now bring our intentions before the Spirit of Life and pray for the women of the Philippines, of all Asia and for those oppressed anywhere in our world.

In the name of our sisters who are no longer with us, who are widows and orphans, we pray for the uncelebrated martyrs of our country, that they may be at peace now with the Spirit of Life.

All: Spirit of Life, hear the prayer of your people.

Lucia Pavia Ticzon: We pray for the refugees, those among whom our sisters worked, those who have fled persecution, repression and war. May we welcome them, respond to their needs, offer safety and shelter, solidarity and love.

All: Spirit of Life, hear the prayer of your people.

Marjorie Evasco: We pray for ourselves, that the many who have died will not have died in vain, that each of us will work for justice in our homes and country, in our world.

All: Spirit of Life, hear the prayer of your people.

Memorial Offering

(As each gets flowers from bowls passed around, the community recite:)

We are bringing these flowers in remembrance of all women who died in all the wars that men have fought.

We remember the nurses who died tending the wounded soldiers of both sides.

We remember the women who were raped by soldiers of their own country and by invaders, and who were then rejected by their fathers and their brothers and their sons.

We remember the women who died or were wounded because they lived in cities and countrysides where bombs fell out of the sky.

We remember all our sisters who have chosen to become strong warriors, fighting for freedom, change and the loves of their lives.

We remember all our sisters, non-combatants, whose lives were ended or foreshortened or crippled because their fathers and brothers went to war against the fathers and brothers of their sisters in their own land or in another.

We weep for them. We do not forget them. And as we remember them, we dedicate ourselves to making a new world where we and our daughters can live free, a world where our grand-daughters and our sisters' granddaughters and great-granddaugters may look back in wonder at some archaic, almost forgotten time when women died because men went to war.

Bequeathing the Future

Marjorie Evasco: Our memories are the eyes that led us back into the history of strong women whose choices and work sustain our survival. As we dream and work for the future let us recognize the persons with whom we shall share a future of peace and equality. To them we bequeath our vision.

(As representatives of various sectors and groups are called out, they come to the central table to receive copies of the magazine and will light an incense stick.)

Offertorium

Lucia Pavia Ticzon: All good gifts around us
spring from our mother earth
Then thank her now, O thank her now
With song and dance and mirth.

(The fruits and flowers are blessed)

Sr. Mary John Mananzan: Bountiful Mother, we offer to you these good gifts of the earth which you have given to us. Blot out the bitter from our earth and our lives and restore the sweet.

Blessing Each Other

(Each member of the community blesses her friends by placing her/their palm/s on her/their head/s saying:)

Friend: I bless you in memory of our mothers.

Song to Close the Rites

Babae ka
Ani Montano

Babae ka, hinahangaa't sinasamba
Ipinagtatanggol, ikaw nama'y walang laya
Ang daigdig mo'y lagi nang nasa tahanan
Ganda lang ang pakinabang sa buhay walang alam.

Ang pinto ng pag-unlad
Sa 'yo laging nakasara
Harapin mo, buksan mo
Ibangon ang iyong pagkatao
Babae ka.

Kalahati ka ng buhay kung ikaw kaya'y wala
Saan ang buhay ipupunla.

Napatunayan mong kaya mong ipaglaban
Ang iyong karapatan at ganap na kalayaan.

Ang pinto ng pag-unlad
Sa 'yo ngayo'y nakabungad
harapin mo, buksan mo
Ibangon ang iyong pagkatao
Babae ka...

Dahil sa akala ay mahina ka
Halaga mo ay di nakikita
Bisig mo man sa lakas ay kulang
Ngunit sa isip ka biniyayaan
Upang ang tinig mo'y maging mapagpasiya
Upang ikaw ay lumaya
Lumaban ka.

Babae may tungkulin ka
Sa pagpapalaya ng bayan
na siya nating simulain. ૐ

TOWARDS TOTAL LIBERATION
Asian Women's Consultation

Invitation to Worship

Here we are at last, women from Continental Asia - from Hong Kong, India, Japan, Korea, Malaysia, Sri Lanka and the Philippines. Together we have come to articulate our faith reflection on the Asian reality from the viewpoint of Asian women. We hope to work together towards fuller humanity. (Country delegates come forward to pin country tags, offer flowers and light candles.)

Song   Sing a New Song

> Ref. Sing a new song unto the Lord
> Let your song be sung
> from mountains high
> Sing a new song unto the Lord
> Singing alleluia.
>
> Yahweh's people dance for joy
> O come before the Lord
> And play for him on glad tambourines
> And let your trumpet sound. Ref.
>
> Rise, O children, from your sleep
> Your Savior now has come
> He has turned your sorrow to joy
> And filled your soul with song. Ref.
>
> Glad my soul for I have seen
> The glory of the Lord
> The trumpet sounds; the dead shall be raised
> I know my Savior lives. Ref.

This is the opening ritual of the Asian Women's Consultation held in Manila and attended by Women Theologians.

Reader 1: Dear Sisters, come and share the story of life. It is still dark but the signs of the coming dawn of freedom is piercing the horizon.

Reader 2. Come and share the hopes and yearnings of the oppressed peoples for total liberation, for a new future of mutuality and love. Let us accept our brokenness and confess our participation in a system that inhibits the birth of a new people and the full growth of our being.

Reader 3: Come and share the great immortal mother's love that is as big as the world. Let us delve into roots of Creative Love by asserting our true identity and by dispelling the myths and the historically assigned roles so that we may participate in solidarity with the struggle of humankind.

All: Let us stand up and give thanks that we are women. Individually, together, we shall face the challenges before us. Let us be open to one another and to the Spirit of Christ and Mary.

Leader: Today is a re-discovery of who I am
who you are
who we are.

Today we shall see our differences and our common interests. Who are we?

All: We are women created by God, endowed with the capacity to think, feel and love, with the right to love, with weaknesses and anxieties, with aspirations and hopes for full humanity, humble and courageous, faithful and understanding.

Leader: Who are we?

All: We are women from the Third World, aware of our situation. We are struggling to understand and do something about the reality that embraces all of us.

Psalm: Sorrow and Hope for Asian Women
Shogeko Masumoto

All: The day we stop burning with love
people will die of cold.

Side 1:   Our anger and despair
        wordless as they are
    Heavily sink in our thoughts
        day in and day out.

Side 2:   Women, each of us bearing
        burdens, too heavy,
    Pressed, bent and torn apart,
        almost endlessly.

Side 1:   Our desires are intermingled
        with our fear.
    How can we be liberated,
        and when?

Side 2:   Some of us can survive
        only by leaving children
    In hospitals or institutions.
        What heartache we all nurse
        in our depth.

Side 1:   Have we ever been taught
        that each of us is invited
    By the Crucified One
        to experience Limitless Love?

Side 2:   Have we ever had a chance
        to feel God's love
    So overwhelmingly
        in our hearts and minds?

Side 1:   Yes, we are created to love,
        and to live more fully
    In the pouring light
        in our small rooms.

All: Let us then gather our hearts before God
        and cry to Him who is the source of Life.
    You know us, God,
        Let us feel that you really love us,
    Here and now, as we really are,
        in spite of our fear and sorrow.

    In Your love, only in Your love,
        can we stand up and step forward
        with hope.

First Reading Meditation on Luke 1:25
                   Dorothy Soelle

Reader 1: It is written that Mary said
              my soul doth magnify the Lord
              and my spirit hath rejoiced in God my Savior
              for he (sic) hath regarded the low estate
                  of his (sic) handmaiden
              for behold from henceforth
              all generations shall call me blessed

Reader 2: Today we express that differently
              my soul sees the land of freedom
              my spirit will leave anxiety behind
              the empty faces of women will be filled with
                  life
              we will become human beings
              long awaited by the generations sacrificed
                  before us

Reader 1: It is written that Mary said
              for he (sic) that is mighty hath done to me
                  great things
              and holy is his (sic) name
              and his (sic) mercy is on them that fear him (sic)
              from generation to generation

Reader 2: Today we express that differently
              the great change that is taking place in us
                  and through us
              will reach all—or it will not take place
              charity will come about when the oppressed
              can give up their wasted lives
              and learn to live themselves

Reader 1: It is written that Mary said
              he (sic) shewed strength with his (sic) arm
              he (sic) hath scattered the proud
              he (sic) hath put down the mighty from their
              seats and exalted them of low degree

Reader 2: Today we express that differently
              we shall dispossess our owners
              and we shall laugh at those
              who claim to understand feminine nature
              the rule of males over females will end

objects will become subjects
they will achieve their own right

Reader 1: It is written that Mary said
he (sic) hath filled the hungry with good things
and the rich he (sic) hath sent away
empty-handed
he (sic) hath holpen his (sic) servant Israel
in remembrance of his (sic) mercy

Reader 2: Today we express that differently
women will go to the moon
and sit in parliaments
their desire for self-determination
will be fulfilled
their fears will be unnecessary
and exploitation will come to an end

Song Ang Puso Ko'y Nagpupuri
(the Magnificat in Pilipino)

Ang puso ko'y nagpupuri
Nagpupuri sa panginoon
Nagagalak ang aking espiritu
Sa aking tagapagligtas.

Second Reading All Sleeping Women Wake Up and Move
Sun Ai Park

Side 1: A stone is thrown
into a calm lake
and the stone made waves
spreading, reaching the far end

Side 2: Let us throw stones
into a deadly calm lake
no matter which edge of the lake
no matter how small the stone
no matter how small the wave

Side 2: The lake is like the world
The lake is like people's minds
The lake is like sisterhood
The lake is like human bondage
The late is like chains of oppression
And the lake is like many others

Side 2:   The stone brings awakening
The wave is a movement
And the movement spreads

All: When all of us
who stand together around the lake
keep throwing our little stones
the wave will never be ceased
the wave will never be ceased
til the whole lake
starts bubbling with life
til the whole lake
makes its own spring
to keep its life going.

**Final
Prayer:**   God of Exodus
God of Liberation
God of Deborah, Judith and Huldah
God of Mary
God our Mother and Father
God the spirit
God of wisdom
Be with us.

Amen. ❁

GO TELL EVERYONE

Asian Women's Consultation

Songs

I.   We are one in bond of love (2x)
      We have joined our spirit with the Spirit of God
      We are one in bond of love

      Let us sing out everyone
      Let us feel our love begin
      Let us join our hands that the world may know
      We are one in the bond of love.

II.   One of us can't fight patriarchy
      Two of us can't fight patriarchy.

            Ref.   But if two and two and fifty make a million
                    We'll see that day come 'round (2x)

      One of us can't fight prostitution
      Two of us can't fight prostitution. *Ref.*

      One of us can't fight oppression
      Two of us can't fight oppression. *Ref.*

      One of us can't fight sexism
      Two of us can't fight sexism. *Ref.*

      One of us can't start a movement
      Two of us can't start a movement. *Ref.*

Responsorial Prayer: Empower us, O God

Reader 1: When James came ashore,he saw a great crowd:

This is the closing ritual of the Asian Women's Consultation held in Manila and attended by Women Theologians.

and his heart went out to them. As the day wore on, his disciples came up to him and said, "This is a lonely place and it is getting very late; send the people off to the farms and villages round about to buy themselves something to eat." "Give them something to eat yourselves," he answered... (Mt. 14:14-15). *(Silence)*

Lord, we remember the millions in our world who must go hungry today, all those who do not have the necessities of life, and for whom life itself has become a burden...

All: Out of the depths we cry to you, Lord,
            Hear our cry and listen to our prayer.

Reader 2:   Jesus was left alone with the woman who remained standing there. He looked up and said, "Woman, where are they? Has no one condemned you?" "No one, sir," she replied. "Neither do I condemn you," said Jesus, "go away, and sin no more." (Jn 8:9-11) *(Silence)*

Lord, we remember all those who, because of their caste or class, color or gender are exploited or marginalized... the forces of oppression that trample on people and the unjust systems which break the spirit of people and rob them of their rights and dignity.

All: Out of the depths we cry to you, Lord,
            Hear our cry and listen to our prayer.

Reader 3: Now a priest happened to be travelling down the road, but when he saw the man, he passed the other way... (Lk 10:31).

Lord, we bring before you the churches and the Christian people around the world. We often have remained silent, passing the other way; often we have been indifferent, often we have been part of the forces that destroy life.

All: Out of the depths we cry to you, Lord,
            Hear our cry and listen to our prayer.

Reader 4: Pilate now took Jesus and had him flogged; and the soldiers plaited a crown of thorns and placed it around his head, and robed him in a purple cloak... He asked Jesus, "Where have you come from?" Pilate said. "Surely you know that I have the authority to crucify you..." (Jn 19:1-2, 9-10). *(Silence)*

Lord we call to mind all authority that treat people as nobodies — military regimes and dictatorships, lonely prisons and unjust laws; the war industry and political greed.

All: Out of the depths we cry to you, Lord.
          Hear our cry and listen to our prayer.

Reader 5: Jesus stood up to read. He opened the scroll and he found the passage which says, "The spirit of the Lord is upon me; He has sent me to announce good news to the poor, to proclaim release for prisoners and recovery of sight for the blind, to let the broken victims go free, to proclaim the year of the Lord's favor." (Lk 4:15-19) *(Silence)*

Lord, we affirm with hope your presence in the world. You see the wounded and the broken, and say — "These are my brothers and sisters."

All: Lord, inspire us with your love
          Challenge us with your truth
          Empower us with your strength
          To live for life in the midst of death. Amen.

Song: We shall overcome (2x)
          We shall overcome someday
          Deep in my heart, I do believe
          We shall overcome someday

          We shall live in peace (2x)...

Reading: Matthew 13:31-32

Song: Women's Solidarity Song

          The songs we sing, not for ourselves
          For those who are oppressed and chained
          Build up a new society
          Let's share and feel with them

          The way we work, not for ourselves
          For those who are oppressed and poor
          Suffer with them and let us know
          That our struggle will win

Come, women unite, be one
Pull out injustice from this world
Live with people, build together
One day we'll reach a new just world

The life we own, not for ourselves
Women and men, work hand in hand
The unity will triumph
We share the vision and hope

Song: Go tell everyone

God's spirit is in my heart.
God has called me and set me apart
This is what I have to do, what I have to do.

God sent me to bring the good news to the poor,
Tell prisoners that they are prisoners no more,
Tell blind people they can see,
And set the downtrodden free.
(And go tell everyone the news
That the kingdom of God has come.) 2x

Leader: Go in peace and proclaim to the world the wonderful
works of God who has brought you LIBERATION. ✿

ABOUT THE AUTHORS

RAYMOND JOSE M. ABOG. An editor of *IBON Databank*, Mr. Abog holds an undergraduate degree in economics from De La Salle University and is taking up his Master's degree in literature at the University of the Philippines.

MARY GRACE AMPIL-TIRONA. A Professor of history and political science at Ateneo de Manila, Ms. Tirona is taking her Ph.D. in Philippine History at the University of the Philippines. Her M.A. is in Asian Studies and she has been an East-West Center Scholar, as well as Project Coordinator of the World Health Organization Learning Center. She is a member of Teresa Makabayan and KAIBA, and board member of The Institute of Women's Studies.

PIA CRISOSTOMO ARBOLEDA. Editor of the Malate Literary Journal feminist issue, Ms. Arboleda was a Fellow at the 16th UP National Writers Workshop. The former secretary general of SAMAKA-GABRIELA, she is taking up her Master's degree in Philippine Studies at De La Salle University. She is administrative assistant and faculty member of The Institute of Women's Studies.

ASIAN WOMEN'S CONSULTATION. An international women's conference attended by women theologians.

SR. MARY KRISTIA BACANI, OSB. Sr. Kristia is a former history and education faculty member. She is St. Scholastica's College AVC Head and Dean of Student Affairs for SY 1988-89.

SR. MARY BELLARMINE BERNAS, OSB. Sr. Bellarmine is the President of St. Scholastica's College, and Executive Director of the Association of Benedictine Schools. She is Corporate Executive Director of the Research and Development Foundation. Treasurer of the PAASCU Board of

Trustees, and member of the Board of Trustees of St. Scholastica's College and Maryknoll College Foundation. Among her organizational affiliations are Concerned Women of the Philippines and KULASA.

SR. HILDA BUHAY, OSB. Sr. Hilda is a Benedictine sister and was a delegate in the Asian Women's Consultation. She now resides in Spain and works with migrant workers.

ROY CHIEFE. A candidate for the priesthood, Roy has been involved with a basic ecclesial community before going for full time theological studies at the Maryhill School of Theology.

SUSAN P. EVANGELISTA. Dr. Evangelista has Masteral degrees in English (University of Wisconsin-Madison) and Asian Studies, and a doctorate in Philippine Studies (University of the Philippines). A professor of Ateneo de Manila, she teaches Asian civilization, English and Indian literature and was Chairperson of the Interdisciplinary Studies Program from 1982 to 1988. She is also a member of the Manila Zen Center and has spent two months visiting ashrams in India.

MARJORIE M. EVASCO. Author of *Dreamweavers*, a book of poems, Ms. Evasco is dedicated to the use of language for women's empowerment. She is De La Salle University Press Director and teaches literature at DLSU.

SR. VIRGINIA FABELLA, MM. Sr. Virginia is currently Coordinator for the Asian Region at the Ecumenical Association of Third World Theologians (EATWOT). She is a member of the Association of Women in Theology (AWIT), FIDES, and THRUST. She was formerly Provincial of the Maryknoll Sisters in the Philippines and Chairperson of the Association of Major Religious Superiors of Women in the Philippines.

SR. MYRNA FRANCIA, ICM. Before enrolling at Maryhill School of Theology for full time studies, Sister Myrna had been living and working with urban poor in Bagong Barrio Caloocan where she worked at the labor desk of the parish.

SR. HELEN GRAHAM, MM. Sr. Helen belongs to the Maryknoll Sisters order and has stayed in the Philippines since 1967. She conducts various seminars at the Sister Formation Institute and also delivers lectures throughout Asia. She handled the "Woman and the Bible" component in SSC's

Women's Studies cognate. Among her recent publications is an article in the book. *Religion and Society.*

MARGARET LACSON. Ms. Lacson works with the EATWOT Asian office in Manila and is a member of AWIT. She is a student at the Maryhill School of Theology.

ARCHE LIGO. A faculty member of the Women's Studies Program, Ms. Ligo has been chairperson of St. Scholastica's College Theology Department. She will soon serve as Assistant Dean of Student Affairs and is a member of WOMB, AWIT and EATWOT.

SR. MARY JOHN MANANZAN, OSB. The National Chairperson of GABRIELA, a national federation of women's organizations, Sr. Mary John is also Dean of the College at St. Scholastica's and Coordinator of The Institute of Women's Studies. She co-founded the Citizen's Alliance for Consumer Protection, of which she is presently Secretary General, and the Center for Women's Resources, of which she is presently Chairperson of the Board of Advisors.

LINA SAGARAL REYES. The poet who wrote *Honing Weapons,* Ms. Reyes works full time as curator of the Contemporary Art Museum of the Philippines (CAMP). She is a graduate of Silliman University where she was the first woman president of the Student Council.

WOMEN INVOLVED IN CREATING CULTURAL ALTERNATIVES (WICCA). A collective of women creative writers, WICCA was launched March 4, 1988.

LOURDES SAN AGUSTIN, KA ODENG, SR. JANNIE, SR. ESTER, YASMIN FLORES, ECO, SR. ROSE and **KARLA FRANCISCO** are pseudonyms belonging to women who chose to share their stories with other women. They are portraits of women who are dedicated to the struggle for empowerment.

Also in the Women's Studies Series

ESSAYS ON WOMEN

Sr. Mary John Mananzan, OSB, Editor

The Filipino Woman Before and After the Spanish
Conquest
    Sr. Mary John Mananzan, OSB

Do Women Really Hold Up Half the Sky?
    Aida F. Santos Maranan

Women's Organizations Offshoots of
National, Political Movements
    Maita Gomez

The Filipinas Have Come and They're
Still Coming
    Marra PL. Lanot

The Woman Problem: Gender, Class
and State Oppression

    Cynthia Nolasco

Gender Ideology and the Status of
Women in a Philippine Rural Community
    Carolyn Israel-Sobritchea

Child Prostitution: Image of a Decadent Society
    Susan Fernandez-Magno

Women in Advertisement
    Pennie Azarcon

Mission of Women in the Church in Asia
    Sr. Virginia Fabella, MM